Be ICONIC!

[signature]

*To Gerard Mauvis in thanks
for his integrity and his inspiration*

CONTENTS

INTRODUCTION

With tears forming in his eyes, the CEO of the once-distinctive and revered company slowly took the stage for the press conference. The organization he served was founded the same year President Lincoln was assassinated. Yet, in its long and storied history, there had never been a moment like this one.

As he sat on the dais, he must have noticed many of his colleagues scattered around the room. Several were already sobbing in anticipation of the announcement that they knew was forthcoming.

Their company—named for a local river—began when a mining engineer established a small ground wood pulp mill. Over the years, the company received countless accolades for anticipating—and regularly driving—marketplace change. It frequently had been named as a global leader. Those descriptors were a thing of the past.

From that initial pulp mill, the company added electricity generation to its portfolio, then expanded to become a major manufacturer of galoshes—those weatherproof rubber boots that slip over your shoes to protect them from water. The company had long been a model of both innovation and adaptation. In the 1930s, they merged with a Finnish rubber company. As regional, then global demand for infrastructure grew, the company became a leader in the cable and wiring industry—essential for transmitting not only electricity but also telephone and telegraph communications.

The company diversified its pulp production and soon became a key producer of various paper products. The rubber business continued to grow as they made everything from bicycle tires to footwear. The cable division expanded as well, and they began manufacturing television sets.

The company had once flirted with bankruptcy, due to the political and economic devastation in the aftermath of World War I. After the Second World War, however, business rebounded—partly by providing the then Soviet Union with the cables required to rebuild their country. This effort also provided a cornerstone for the organization's future growth.

The company's visionary leaders recognized the potential of telecommunications—even though that division operated at a loss for many years. They poured resources into a digital switching product that became an industry standard for telephone equipment in early network architecture. Their engineers even developed a mobile telephone network that provided 100 percent coverage to their home nation—in 1978.

For a long time, many people marveled at how adept and adroit the organization and its leaders were. The company created a new tool for mobile networking—cellular handsets—that were used by everyone from global trendsetters to average workers. They expanded into products such as computers and high-quality displays. After divesting itself of its formative businesses—paper, tires, footwear, and various consumer electronics—the company's decision makers chose to concentrate exclusively on one industry: telecommunications.

This company that started from humble origins became a global icon.

That day at the press conference, however, none of those achievements were being celebrated. Instead, the CEO was about to address the more recent failures. Relative startups were running rings around the company's operating software. The CEO had recently sent a memo to employees describing the team as being on a "burning platform" in a "war." The mobile devices the company released—once viewed as the vanguard of technology and scooped up by the tens of millions—languished on the shelves as customers bolted for easier-to-use alternatives.

In 2013, after a long downward spiral, the company that enjoyed a rich tradition and iconic standing for almost 150 years was being acquired—bailed out, in actuality—

by a business that had about one-fourth of the longevity and history. At this press conference, Nokia CEO Stephen Elop announced that Microsoft was purchasing his company.

As he looked over the assembled crowd of reporters and his colleagues, Elop attempted to address the spectacular failure of the global icon he led. He gave his take on what had decimated the formerly successful conglomerate, as well as the events that presaged the termination of about half of the company's employees.

"We didn't do anything wrong," he tearfully and defiantly claimed. "But somehow we lost."

Maybe Mr. Elop's inflated compensation clouded his judgment. It is hard to imagine that such a highly remunerated global executive would think that he didn't do *anything* wrong while at the helm as a distinctive company lost its iconic status.

Maybe Mr. Elop totally missed the mark. Perhaps Nokia lost its iconic status because of mismanagement, because of poor organizational focus.

There is no doubt that *attaining* success is critical. However, knowing the steps to *sustain* and *regain* it are vital as well. Could it be that Nokia's leadership knew how to create their lofty status in the marketplace—

but not how to preserve their position, or reclaim it once it was lost?

That question is the one I've been pondering for the past several years. When I wrote a book on how to create distinction, I did not focus on how a leader or an organization maintained or enhanced the marketplace advantages they generated. A few years after teaching people how to make their company stand out, I had a blinding flash of the obvious. I realized that I now needed to focus on how to sustain, or possibly regain, the distinction they had created.

As I spoke at corporate events on the elements of setting yourself apart from the competition in the marketplace, it became clear that there was another level beyond distinction—beyond setting your company apart—that extraordinary leaders and organizations could attain as well. The companies that are widely recognized and frequently used as illustrations of "best practices" (some to the point their example has become clichéd) are not merely distinctive. They are much more than that!

For instance, Samsung has created distinction—and left many other mobile device manufacturers, such as LG, HTC, and Motorola, eating their dust. Apple, however, is on a higher level. It isn't merely distinctive. It has become iconic.

Your local neighborhood probably has a coffee shop that stands above the rest because of its customer experience or a special blend that attracts java enthusiasts. That little local store has found a way to create distinction. Starbucks, however, is iconic.

Apple and Starbucks are global companies, yet worldwide recognition is not a requirement for iconic status. For example, there is a plethora of steakhouses. Some national chains—Del Frisco's, Morton's, Fleming's—have risen to the point of distinction. St. Elmo's, however, is iconic. You may not have heard of St. Elmo's if you have never been to Indianapolis. It is the place where almost every visitor to the city wants to go. In downtown Indy, none of the distinctive national brands are even in the same ballpark in terms of recognition—or revenue. It has become a model for all types of businesses in the region—not just restaurants. (You'll learn much more about St. Elmo's in the concluding chapter of this book.)

As the Nokia example powerfully illustrates, attaining iconic status does not ensure that lofty perch will be maintained.

Think of Sears, Arthur Andersen, MCI, Lehman Brothers, Wachovia, Saab, Compaq Computers, JC Penney, and Abercrombie & Fitch. This is just a short list of companies that have disappeared or are in significant difficulty, even though they had been well known and highly respected. Certainly, we could debate if a company like Wachovia was iconic or simply distinctive. Nonetheless, every one of these organizations—and their respective leaders—were perceived to be powerhouses at one period or another (and some for a very long time.)

So how does a local steakhouse like St. Elmo's maintain and even enhance their iconic status since 1902 while these formidable global organizations fail? Or as an executive in the hospitality industry at one of the most incredible resort properties in the United States asked me, "How can we move from great to distinctive to a truly iconic hotel?" Perhaps you want to learn how to stand out from your competition and enhance market-place advantages. It could be that you've enjoyed a degree of success in setting yourself apart and now you want to move to the highest level.

Or maybe you have already achieved iconic status and you're ruminating on how you can keep your standing from slipping through your corporate or professional fingers.

Great is not good enough in today's hypercompetitive marketplace. With all the technological advances in the past decade, starting a business has never been easier. That means being distinctive has never been more diffi-cult. And, unfortunately, distinction may not provide all of the extraordinary advantages it formerly did for you and your company.

I researched my first book on distinction because I could not find any significant advice on how to make my own business stand out. I used what I learned to grow my own small enterprise and help others create their own distinction. Now, there are so many authors and speakers helping businesses and individuals stand out from the competition that it's hard for even the so-called thought leaders to stand out from *their* competition.

Since then I've come to the realization that standing out isn't good enough anymore. How can you possibly succeed if nothing that you offer engages your customers or prospects—or inspires your employees to deliver the results they desire?

Let's face it, you do not want to be the CEO speaking at a press conference, or the entrepreneur standing in front of your employees, or the sales manager addressing your team, naively and defiantly insisting that despite the fact that your people are losing their jobs and your company is now toast—you did *nothing* wrong.

That is why it's time for you to become *iconic*!

How to Get the Most Out of This Book

This book has three goals. To help you...

1) **Attain iconic status.**

   What does it take to be perceived not merely as *distinctive* within your specific field or industry—but also recognized as a significant organization or professional across a wide spectrum?

2) **Maintain and enhance that status once you've achieved it.**

   You've often heard that once you're out front, you also have a target on your back. After you've made it to iconic status, what do you do to maintain and enhance your position so you don't get disrupted in a hypercompetitive environment?

3) **Regain that status should you find it has eroded in the marketplace.**

   Perhaps through no fault of your own, you are in a position where your status—and the perception about your relevance in the marketplace—has slipped. Can you regain your previous level of prestige? And, if so, how is that accomplished?

There may be some aspects of this book that challenge your thinking. (I certainly hope so!) Some things you may not have heard at your last business meeting:

- **Go negative for greater success.**
- **"Underpromise/overdeliver" is a horrible way to deal with customers.**
- **There are only two factors by which customers will judge your organization.**
- **There is a single aspect that your organization must cultivate—for if it doesn't, you can't compete.**
- **You need to stop selling your products and services.**
- **If you aren't distinctive locally (meaning in your geographic area or in your specific industry), you can't become iconic.**

You'll also learn some aspects about becoming iconic you may not have previously considered. For example:

- **Iconic companies know there is great room for improvement on the things they already know how to do.**
- **Iconic organizations and leaders have captivated our attention and attained a level that transcends their individual and specific field of endeavor.**

- **Iconic businesses have resolved they will not be reactive to external events outside their control.**
- **Iconic institutions understand that sales metrics can be misleading in terms of organizational growth and achieving their potential.**

To get the most out of this book and attain your target of becoming iconic, you should read this book at least two times.

The first time, read this book straight through and absorb the content and ideas. The second time, review this book with a journal or notebook by your side. Make notes and plans about how you'll implement the concepts I've outlined. For example: the first time through, consider the concepts in the context of how Nokia was fundamentally destroyed as an iconic leader in mobile telephones.

The second time through, ask yourself questions specific to your own situation, such as:

- What am I not seeing in my business?
- Am I obsessing about our own products and services and missing key market indicators?
- What or who could disrupt us the way that Apple and Samsung disrupted Nokia?

READING GROUPS

If you are reading this book, you are likely a leader of a company or organization looking to take your business to the highest level. Even if you are an individual—perhaps an entrepreneur, sales professional, or sole proprietor—wanting to do more than just stand out from the crowd, it is important to note that you should not try to analyze your business and market by yourself. Just as the software sharing company Github utilizes the collective brainpower of hundreds of engineers to accomplish complex tasks in record time, the power of collaboration can have a profoundly significant impact on your business as you analyze your distinction and how to achieve the highest level.

One organization I worked with developed a path to iconic status by forming reading groups. They challenged every person in the company to read a chapter a week. Next, they split into departments and had detailed conversations every Wednesday about how that week's chapter impacted their individual department or team. Finally, they executed tactics every week on one specific change they made based upon the points of a chapter. This was part of their recipe to move from being considered as one of many strong players in their field to becoming an iconic business, respected throughout the world. No matter the size of your business or division, you can do the same.

At the end of each chapter, you'll find a set of questions that will both stimulate your personal thinking and provide discussion starters. I highly recommend you form reading groups in your company or organization and discuss these questions. If you are an individual professional striving for higher achievement, do it with your team, mentors, or friends. This type of collective thinking will have a significant impact on the way you do business. For you to advance your organization (and yourself) through the process, answering these questions precisely—and specifically to your situation—is critical.

If you're familiar with my previous work, the initial part of this new book will be an updated review and expansion on the content you've already consumed. You will likely note a couple of significant changes as well. It's important to reintroduce this information before we move to a higher level.

If you haven't read any of the information and stories that I've provided earlier on creating distinction, don't worry. The next couple of chapters will get you up to speed.

While you may have previously been exposed to some of the information in this book, it is my fervent hope that you won't toss it aside and say, "Ah, I've heard this before." What if Billy Graham would have said, "You've heard this material from the Bible before, so there's no need for me to preach about it again"? What if Steven

Spielberg had said, "There have been movies about aliens out before, so there's no need for me to make *E.T.*"?

Please don't misunderstand me. I am certainly not comparing this book to the Bible or *E.T.* The point I'm attempting to make is that it's not about whether you're familiar with the concepts or not. It's about whether the material that you're absorbing is presented in a manner that compels you to think and act. In other words, even if you've heard it before, I promise you that the themes discussed here are critical to your success—and we all have room for improvement. In fact, every iconic leader and organization knows there is room for improvement on the things they already know how to do.

If you've heard it before but aren't doing anything about it—perhaps, just *perhaps* you need to consider the material once again.

This book presents the best that I can contribute on the topic. I'd love to hear what you think—and how it has been of value to you. Send me a note at: iconic@scott-mckain.com. I promise to personally read every message—and use your input to improve and enhance the content. I would be grateful if you'd take a moment to share.

That is how you will get the most out of this book. *Let's get started!*

PART ONE

WHAT IT MEANS TO BE ICONIC

CHAPTER ONE

WHAT IS AN "ICONIC" ORGANIZATION?

For every Amazon, there is a Sears. For every Apple, there is a Nokia. For every Starbucks, there is a HoJo's. When we mention an iconic company of today, we often forget there was one in the past that was equally dominant.

Remember the goals of this book are to help you or your organization achieve iconic status, maintain that status, and if your reputation has slipped, how you can regain that level of distinction. In this chapter we will examine the Four Levels of Business Distinction and what is so special about those businesses that have attained iconic status.

THE FOUR LEVELS OF BUSINESS DISTINCTION

You may not be as different as you think.

On a recent flight I enjoyed a brief conversation with the person sitting next to me. As we landed at our destination, my seatmate turned to me and presented her business card. Coincidentally, I discovered that she was involved in a similar business to the one my late wife, Sheri, worked in for many years. Naturally, I was interested in knowing more about her organization, so when I got home I looked up her company's website. The headline I saw there—What Makes Us Different—really struck me. As I'm fascinated by elements that make any organization stand out from their competition, I read the four bullet points listing the aspects that her company believed were the ones separating them from the others in their industry.

- experience
- depth of knowledge
- founded by innovative entrepreneurs
- depth in multiple market segments

I thought about each point on this list. *Experience* is just longevity. It's as if they're suggesting their competitors are staffed with rookies who have no background. Using the same logic, when they say *depth of knowledge* makes them unique, it seems they're asserting the competition is dumber than they are. The fact that they are *founded by innovative entrepreneurs* doesn't strike me as an extraordinary trait since, by definition, every business had to be founded by an entrepreneur. I guess their competition was started by unimaginative entrepreneurs. Finally, the company claimed to have *depth in multiple market segments.* My wife said the same thing about the company where she worked in the late nineties. I promise you this is nothing new or unique.

None of these points make the company *different.* There is absolutely zero here that would truly qualify to be listed under the heading What Makes Us *Different!* These points merely make that company moderately *relevant* in the hypercompetitive industry in which they play.

Could you be making
the same mistake?

If you and your rival are both claiming
that your great service is what makes
you different, then from the customer's
perspective you *aren't.*

This company has inadvertently displayed that they don't get it. They don't understand what would make their customers perceive them as superior to the competition.

If your prospects think that you don't understand your own uniqueness, wouldn't they also surmise that you might not grasp other salient aspects of doing business together? And just because you say it is so doesn't make it so.

You cannot attain differentiated,
distinctive, or iconic status by demand.

In other words, no individual or organization can stand up and announce, "We are iconic, dammit!" Well, I guess they could—but based solely upon their declaration, no one else would recognize them as such.

Obtaining iconic status happens only through hard and smart work that leads to overwhelmingly enthusiastic evaluations from your customers in a competitive marketplace. Attaining the highest level of distinction is something that you attain because you have *attracted* it—not because you have demanded it.

There are too many companies and a multitude of professionals proclaiming they stand out from the competition. What they evidently fail to recognize is that the *marketplace* decides their status—not them.

I'm acquainted with—and a big fan of—the iconic Fox Sports personality Colin Cowherd. One of the segments on Colin's show that I love is, "Where Colin was right, where Colin was wrong." He presents a few of the predictions and opinions that he's previously expressed, then he reviews where he was on target and analyzes where he missed the mark.

Well, in reviewing my previous book, *Create Distinction*, I confess that there was a point where I missed the mark. I wrote about the three levels of business distinction. However, after sharing the concept with thousands of leaders, I realize now that I failed to recognize a fourth level. Ironically, it is the most significant level of all.

Let's first examine the Four Levels of Business Distinction. Then, I'll help you evaluate where you fall on that spectrum, so you can design your plan to elevate your standing.

Level 1: Sameness

Do customers perceive a compelling difference between you and your competition on something other than price? Do they see you as something more than a commodity? If not, you fall into the first level of business distinction: sameness. This, I believe, is the worst spot in which any organization or professional can reside.

Years ago, I had a manager tell me that customers were loyal to his company's product because, "We are the cheapest in the market and that's what customers are looking for—the lowest price." I explained that his customers weren't attached to his product; they were just committed to being cheap. All his competitors had to do was start selling a similar product at a lower price and his customers would run for the door.

The problem for this manager—and many like him—is that it seems to be easier to keep cranking out what we've been doing for years than to try to move up into a higher station. Many people think that continuing to do what's worked in the past will continue to be safe. This approach isn't safe at all. In fact, it's the most unsound and unhealthy place to be. At this level—where margins are small and competition is intense—the failure to provide an aspect that sets you apart from your competition can be deadly.

LEVEL 2: DIFFERENTIATION

When customers perceive there is something about your product or service that is unique from the competition, you have differentiated yourself in the marketplace. It simply draws more attention to you and your efforts. In addition, customers are willing to pay more for products or services that have some aspect that sets them apart from the swarm of the similar.

This approach works for individuals as they seek to grow their career as well. The professional who has something special about her background, knowledge, or approach will naturally find her talents more highly valued than one who has taken the same path as the horde of others seeking advancement.

The challenge here, however, is that it is easy to presume that mere differentiation translates into superiority. It doesn't.

Different is not better.
Different is just different.

As I've noted many times, if I slap every customer in the face, I am different. That does *not* mean I am better.

Does "why" make you differentiated?

There is a lot of discussion these days about a little word *Why*. In 2009, business consultant Simon Sinek wrote a megabestselling book *Start with Why* in which he espouses that we start by asking why questions:

- Why are we in business?
- Why do we get out of bed in the morning?
- Why does our company exist?

Many entrepreneurs, business leaders, and professionals began asking themselves about the *why* of their business or their careers. Sinek instructed his readers to use their *why* as the foundation upon which they will differentiate themselves in the marketplace. He suggests when we do this, we begin the process of becoming more valuable.

I agree that *why* is a great question to ask yourself. It is one that can lead to higher levels of understanding and insight that can be important to your personal and professional journeys. It requires deeper thinking about your purpose and priorities.

Sinek takes it a bit further, though. He advocates that people don't buy *what* you do; they buy *why* you do it.

On this point, I respectfully but fervently disagree.

For instance, the burgers at Shake Shack are unbelievably good. They are so tasty, I believe that is what differentiates Shake Shack from the standard burger competition. As their customer, I don't give a damn *why* they make them so delicious—I just care that they *do*.

Author, speaker, and close friend Joe Calloway has brilliantly observed that even at a company like Apple (one that Sinek cites as a primary example of starting with the *why*), this approach does not work. "Go into any Apple store," Calloway says, "and ask an employee at the Genius Bar why he is there. He likely won't cite any Apple corporate mantra. Instead, he'll probably say it's to pay off his student loans."

"In any business—large or small—there are many varied 'whys,'" Calloway continues. "People buy what you *do*—and, more importantly, *how well you do it*. The key is not the 'why,' it's to be the best at what matters most to customers."

> *Problems in differentiation are usually not about your* why, *it's that you need to deliver a better* how.

In many of the organizations I've observed, three of the most frequently asked *how* questions are:

- How do we sell more?
- How do we cut overhead?
- How do we enhance our profits?

Notice what all these statements have in common? *They're all inwardly focused.*

What if, instead, we asked questions like:

- How can we be of greater service to our customers?
- How can we make the experience of doing business with us more compelling?
- How will the steps we are taking impact the prospects we want to convert to clients?

While Sinek states the *how* is important in everyday decision making—and that your *how* should align with your *why*—there's a critical difference that I've noted among iconic companies and leaders.

Disney is unquestionably an iconic company. Through the leadership of CEO and Chairman Bob Iger, it continues to navigate the difficult waters of the changing media and entertainment environment. So what is the *why* of Disney?

Perhaps in an earlier time, one could say Disney was in business to create, promote, and distribute family entertainment. But now they own or have a controlling interest in, among other ventures, ESPN, A&E Network, Hyperion Books, Reedy Creek Energy Services, ABC Television Network. So how do they define their *why* in today's world? None of those subsidiaries is devoted exclusively to family entertainment.

"If you want to thrive in a disrupted world, you have to be incredibly adept at not standing still," Iger told *Vogue* magazine.[1] It would be very difficult to pivot as quickly and move as rapidly as Iger suggests if you're dogmatically focused on an esoteric *why* as opposed to the more practical *how*.

If a customer decides to do more business with you, which of these two comments do you suppose is most likely to express the reason for their choice:

- "I like *why* they are in business."
- "I like *how* they do what they do better."

Moving from level one to level two does not commence with asking *why*. Instead, it begins with creating and executing a better *how*.

> *Differentiation based upon the quality of how you do what you do lifts you above the level of sameness.*

LEVEL 3: DISTINCTION

Once you have differentiated yourself or your company from the competition, it is time to become distinct. There are some organizations that have attained a higher level of differentiation from those with which they compete. They have created an advantage of such an extraordinary level of significance that customers are attracted to them. This is the essence of distinction.

Pursuit versus Attraction

Companies and individuals that have not created distinction in their marketplace have to pursue their customers. Unfortunately, the problem they encounter is that there is a fundamental difference between pursuit and attraction. Please don't misunderstand—I'm not talking about some New Age "law of attraction." Instead, I'm referring to the viewpoint of late business philosopher Jim Rohn, mentor of famed motivational speaker, Tony Robbins.

Rohn said that "success is something you attract, not something you pursue."[2] If you choose the path of pursuit, you might constantly be chasing after an elusive objective. Rohn espoused growing your value as a person and a professional to such a significant level that you would attract more opportunities and, therefore, have a greater chance of becoming more successful.

Yet, many organizations and leaders simply set the bar too low. They exhort their teams to close the next deal or build a better product or deliver a better service without ever contemplating what it would mean if they would truly become distinctive.

Ask Phil Mickelson what his goal might be for any tournament in which he is entered. Do you think he would *ever* say, "Gee, I hope to make the cut"?

Ask LeBron James what his goal is for an approaching NBA season. Do you think he would ever say, "I think that maybe we can make the playoffs"?

Yet, sales professionals seek to grow their performance by 2 percent. Customer service leaders hope to enhance their Net Promoter Scores by a few points. C-suite executives set a target to improve EBITDA by a modest amount.

Are you so busy pursuing
customers that you haven't considered
what might *attract* them?

Customers and employees that you attract
typically become much more valuable than
those you've had to pursue.

Incremental improvements add up over time. And you must realistically assess your current situation to set targets that are meaningful for the immediate future. However, here's another point we must understand: champions think like champions. They invest whatever is required to get there.

That's part of the challenge for many professionals and organizations. It's much easier to say, "We're going to grow our Net Promoter Score by 2 percent," than it is to commit to delivering an Ultimate Customer Experience (more on this later) so we become the standard by which others are judged. It's more common to say you're going to grow sales by a certain percentage than it is to do what it takes to create distinction.

Never forget the high price champions
pay to become the distinctive best.

Have you set the bar too low? It's a critical question we must all ask ourselves—and be honest in our response. You cannot play small and simultaneously attain the level of distinction.

In the next chapter, we'll review the four cornerstones of distinction. You cannot reach iconic status without first becoming distinct. For now, it's time to look at the highest level of business distinction.

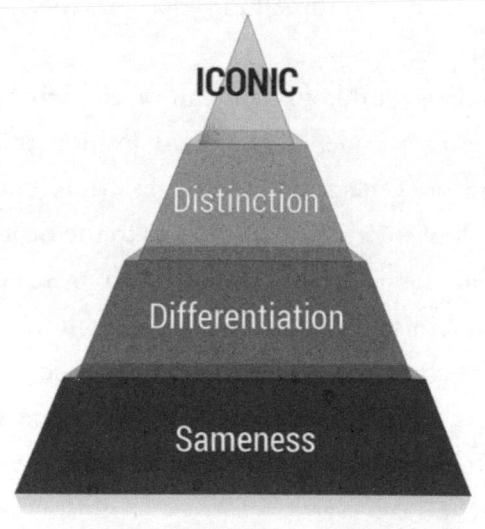

LEVEL 4: ICONIC

The ultimate level of distinction for any organization or leader to attain is to become iconic.

Today, we may think of icons as the small symbols on our phone or desktop that denotes an application or document. The word was first used in that sense in 1982. The root of the word *icon*, however, is much older. *Icon* originally came from the Greek *eikon* meaning "likeness, image, or portrait." In the sixteenth century, the Latin word *ikon* was used by the churches—particularly the Eastern Orthodox Church—as the word for depictions of Jesus or other important Christian figures in oil paintings or wooden panels.

Whether you think of the ancient *eikon* or the religious ikons or today's digital icons, they are all symbols that represent something that has been deemed important.

In today's world, an icon can be everything from a movie star to a leader of the latest fashion trends. For example, every generation has its iconic entertainers who are symbols of their times: from Elvis to the Beatles, from Michael Jackson to Jay-Z, from John Wayne to Al Pacino, from Tom Cruise to Dwayne "The Rock" Johnson. Likewise, throughout the years there are iconic companies and leaders: from GE and Jack Welch to Apple and Steve Jobs, from Berkshire Hathaway and Warren Buffett to Microsoft and Bill Gates.

*Performers, organizations, and leaders
became iconic when they move from
being distinctive in their respective
marketplaces to becoming broadly
recognized as captivating.*

If you're into rap music, you probably know Dolla $ign, XXXTentacion, and Migos—all of whom have top ten songs on the charts at the writing of this chapter. If that style of music doesn't suit your tastes, you probably have never heard of them. However, if you know nothing about rap—even if you abhor it—you likely have heard of Jay-Z. While the first three rappers I mentioned can fill clubs with fans, Jay-Z can sell out arenas and stadiums—in part, because he has transcended his specific genre of music. He is iconic.

I'm a big fan of Ray Dalio, the billionaire investor and hedge fund manager who recently authored a terrific bestselling book, *Principles: Life and Work.*

Despite Dalio's incredible financial track record and a *Forbes* estimated net worth of $17.4 billion dollars, I will bet the farm that he's nowhere nearly as well known as the Oracle of Omaha, Warren Buffett. It's not just Buffett's greater wealth—estimated at $84.7 billion—that makes him iconic. His status is not exclusively because he owns companies that the masses do business with daily— Geico, Duracell, and Dairy Queen. While Dalio is distinctive in the world of finance, Buffett is iconic because his seeming accessibility to the public and down-home attributes have transcended his specific field.

Therefore, the fundamental difference is this:

Iconic organizations and leaders have captivated our attention and attained a level that transcends their specific field of endeavor.

Iconic organizations and leaders have become such universal symbols of distinction they are not only irresistible to customers in their marketplace, they compel interest and admiration across a wide spectrum.

At the risk of sounding like the professor whom I had for a class on logic in college, you can become distinctive and not attain the level of iconic. However, you cannot become iconic without first reaching the level of distinction.

The next chapter will get you up to—and through—the first step: creating distinction.

Questions for Chapter 1

Take some time to go through these questions with your team, study group, or mentor. Share ideas and insights that will help you drill deeper into the strategies and tactics that can apply to your specific organization.

- At which level of distinction would I currently place my organization or department (or myself)? Why?
- What level do I reasonably believe that my organization or department (or that I personally) could attain? Why?
- What are the specific points of differentiation that customers or others would recognize about us?
- Are we distinctive within our industry or field? Why or why not?
- If we are distinctive, what do we need to do to become iconic? If we aren't distinctive, what could we do to attain that level?

CHAPTER TWO

THE FOUR CORNERSTONES OF DISTINCTION

THE ORIGINS OF DISTINCTION

After my first wife, Sheri, passed away from ovarian cancer in 2005, I had to hitch up my pants and get to work. Left with an enormous amount of debt from medical bills and more, I found myself in a floundering financial status. At the same time, I was emotionally devastated and adrift. As her sole caregiver, I had cut back on my speaking to stay home with her. Now, I had to jump back into a hypercompetitive market and try to reestablish my professional speaking career.

At that point, if someone asked, "What do you talk about?" my answer was usually, "Oh, about an hour." In other words, I had made my reputation as a proficient speaker on any number of generic topics. You name it, I probably had a speech for it: sales, leadership, customer service, motivation, team building, time management—just to name a few.

The first step to rebuilding my career was to contact the speakers bureaus that had previously been a primary source of my bookings. I wanted to let them know I was back in gear and ready to work with them again. During the conversation with the first bureau I contacted, I asked a simple question: "When you recommend me to your clients, what do you say about me?"

The immediate response was, "We say that you are a great speaker and a really nice guy!"

While the person on the other end of the line thought they were giving me a great compliment, I was nothing short of *horrified*! I've worked at my craft, and I aspire to be considered a great professional speaker. And don't get me wrong: there's nothing bad about being nice. However, all I could think of was a ridiculous scenario: the vice president of marketing for some major corporation turns to a staff member and says, "You know what we really need for this year's meeting? We need a speaker who is a *really nice guy!*" That would *never* happen! Instead, the staffer would be instructed to find the best speaker on marketing or sales or life balance.

"Great speaker and good gal or guy" was about as generic and unremarkable of a description as I could imagine. What could possibly blend into the background more than that?

Sadly, this conversation played itself out repeatedly with numerous speakers bureaus. My branding—or lack thereof—was "the good speaker who is a really nice guy."

Naturally, I decided that I had to reposition my business. It's hard enough to *position* yourself in a marketplace. That requires a message compelling enough to move people to think about a product or service in a positive manner—and remember that concept. To *reposition* requires a new message so compelling that it makes you forget what you already know—then moves you to consider and remember the new concept in its place.

Initially, I started looking for books that would teach how to stand out and move up in a hypercompetitive marketplace. Jack Trout's book *Differentiate or Die* was excellent, but I wanted something to help me become distinctive—not just different.

That's when it hit me. "If I am having so much difficulty finding this," I asked myself, "what's the likelihood that others are as well?" If I was having trouble making my business stand out from the competition, the odds were good that there had to be more professionals dealing with the same problem. I had found my niche.

My personal pursuit to learn about distinction for my own little company had turned into a quest to research, study, write, and teach organizations and leaders around the world how to become distinct.

The irony doesn't escape me that I've just told you my *why*.

Sales of our company's books on distinction, speeches, virtual training programs, and more have totaled in the millions of dollars. Yet, not one client has ever asked me to explain *why* that's my topic.

Clients have something more important in mind:

How does what you do help them to become better at what they do?

I hope you have a compelling *why*. Certainly, I hope you do not have a *why* that is grounded in tragedy as I do. But always remember—it's the *how* that will make you stand out from the competition.

Let's examine the steps to create distinction in your marketplace—and the *hows* that will ensure your customers perceive that you are on a higher echelon. These *hows* I discovered are the elements that make up the four cornerstones of distinction.

1) CLARITY

Several years ago, I read in the *Wall Street Journal* that Procter & Gamble announced they were getting rid of more than half of their brands. "CEO A.G. Lafley said that P&G will focus on seventy to eighty consumer brands, including Tide and Pampers, which together account for some 90 percent of the company's sales and 95 percent of profits, and either divest or find ways to exit between 90 to 100 smaller brands."[3]

This reminded me of Dr. Sheena Iyengar and her research. Dr. Iyengar, famed Columbia University professor and author of *The Art of Choosing*, is perhaps the world's leading expert on why people select one option over another. (She was featured in Malcolm Gladwell's 2005 book, *Blink*. I'm honored that she has been one of my coaching clients.)

The more options you provide customers, Dr. Iyengar discovered, the more difficult you make it for them to choose any particular one.

The same phenomenon happens internally in organizations. The more brands, options, projects, initiatives, and KPIs you have, the more difficult it becomes to focus with clarity on what really matters for the company.

The first cornerstone of distinction is clarity. Obviously, if you aren't focused, you cannot exemplify the clarity required to stand out from your competition.

Well-known public speaker, leadership consultant, and author Greg McKeown wrote in his book *Essentialism: The Disciplined Pursuit of Less* that "the word *priority* came into the English language in the 1400s. It was singular. It meant the very first or prior thing. It stayed singular for the next 500 years. Only in the 1900s did we pluralize the term and start talking about priorities."[4]

P&G took a step toward clarity—focusing on their brands that are most critical and establishing performance as *the* priority not *a* priority.

If your product line is diffused, it's difficult to gain clarity. And if you're constantly analyzing your *priorities*, consider if you've been specific enough to be perceived as unique in the marketplace.

As you look at your priority and seek to gain clarity, think about your *high concept* statement. The high concept model is one I've been a fan of for a long time, devoting significant space to it in previous books. A basic premise is that if it takes you longer than six seconds to express a thought, idea, or attribute of your product or service, you aren't clear enough on it. A high concept statement is a brutally brief, powerful phrase that will interest and engage the listener.

Going back to P&G, their high concept statement is "We provide branded products and services of superior quality and value that improve the lives of the world's consumers." When they became so diversified, they began providing inferior products under the P&G name. This meant their performance wasn't congruent with their high concept. CEO Lafley realized that had to change.

The idea of a "high concept pitch" originated in Hollywood. Producers have to sell their ideas to studio executives in order to get the funding required to create their television or movie projects. Studio executives hear requests for funding for projects all day, every day. In order to pique their interest, producers had to learn to convey their concepts in six seconds or less. If they could do that, the executives knew the film could be marketed to moviegoers—who don't want to listen to a long explanation of the plot of a movie, either. That's how films like *Snakes on a Plane*—where the high concept line became the actual title—are sold.

Consider the more recent comedic movie, *Blockers*. Imagine the pitch: the producer simply says to a studio executive: "Envision every outrageous teen comedy you've seen—*American Pie, Superbad, Fast Times at Ridgemont High*—only this time we will tell it from the *parent's* point of view."

That high concept statement is brutally brief—it takes six seconds to say, yet is compelling. Every parent has worried or wondered about their teen and all the potential trouble that awaits them in the world. Most of the previous comedies focused on the perspective of teens seeking their independence. This high concept grabs our attention because it moves us to consider a different point of view from what we would expect from a raunchy comedy.

(Perhaps that's why one reviewer wrote, "Beneath the whacking, smutty, in-your-face teen sex farce, *Blockers* is a mature, thoughtful exploration of parental responsibility and the capacity of burgeoning adults to navigate life's difficult choices."[5])

During a break at a conference where I was giving a speech to financial advisors, one professional approached me to ask my opinion about his high concept statement.

"I'll build your financial future!" he exclaimed. I acted as though I were dozing off.

"The problem with that statement," I said, "is that everyone in the room could claim exactly the same thing. It does nothing to make you distinctive. Tell me a little bit about you and your background." It turned out he was a retired Air Force fighter pilot.

Together we came up with his new high concept statement: *I fly people through financial turbulence*. Significantly more interesting, right?

Don't miss the importance of what this statement did for his practice. It's not just catchphrase or tagline. His high concept statement focused his business and made him distinctive. This financial advisor now is clear about his special place in the market. He focuses on risk-averse investors, those who aren't interested in aggressive growth but want safer investments. He's focused. In other words, he's taken the first step in creating a unique practice in financial services—the first step for anyone who wants to be distinctive.

Achieving Clarity is not easy. And it's not exclusively for owners, managers, and leaders. Your entire team must be focused too.

At a consulting day I spent with an IT firm, the owner told me I could move directly to the second of the four cornerstones, as he was certain they required no help with Clarity. I challenged him to tolerate a little exercise with his executive team. I gave each of the six department heads a blank three-by-five-inch notecard. I asked those leaders to write a brief statement on the card that would clearly describe their company and what made it distinctive in their competitive market. When the executives read their statements to the rest of the room, the owner was stunned. Five of the six statements varied widely. The owner simply assumed that because he had Clarity, it was shared by his team. The exercise proved he was wrong.

It doesn't matter if we're talking about a small business or an international conglomerate. If your company's leaders aren't clear about what advantages you have in the marketplace, how in the world do you expect your employees to grasp it? If your employees aren't clear about why someone should buy from you instead of the competition, how can you assume customers get it? Make Clarity a key goal across the company and in the marketplace.

In our next section, we'll expand on this. For now, your goal is to develop a high concept statement for your business, your product or service, your department—and yourself.

Have a high concept statement ready.

Your goal is to be extraordinarily precise
about what makes you stand out to
customers. Create a compelling statement
that requires six seconds or less to convey.

2) CREATIVITY

From the last section, it's easy to understand the clarity
of the high-concept pitch for *Blockers*. However, did you
also notice the creativity? It is, to my knowledge, the
first comedy to approach the coming-of-age theme from
the parents' perspective. (And, as of this writing, it has
earned $90 million at the box office against a production
budget of $21 million.)

Enterprise Rent-A-Car is another excellent example
of creativity. The Ford you rent from Hertz is the same as
the one you drive from Avis. There is zero product variation in the rental car business. Enterprise, however, was
innovative on how they could serve their customer. They
asked, in essence, "What is one thing we can do that is
unique in the rental car experience?" Enterprise decided
to bring the car to the customer rather than make the customer come to them. Since they couldn't rent a different
or better automobile than the competition, they got cre-

ative in how they could connect with their customer. That one point of creativity is essential to why Enterprise has become the biggest player in their industry.

There are two challenges that I consistently encounter when discussing innovation with leaders. They often perceive that

1) Creativity equals chaos, and
2) Being creative is only for startups in the hi-tech industry

First, note that both Enterprise and *Blockers* didn't blow up the model—they just changed a single aspect about it. There was no chaotic disruption, just a mere adjustment. Enterprise brought the car to the customer; *Blockers* looked at the same situation from a different point of view.

In business, any innovation in how you reach or serve your customer can make an enormous difference. And it doesn't even have to be product related—you can be creative in a single aspect of service.

At Moe's Southwest Grill, employees shout, "Welcome to Moe's!" with enthusiasm every time a customer enters the restaurant. As they say on their website, "We're not trying to scare you or anything. Our signature 'Welcome to Moe's' greeting represents our passionate promise to always welcome everyone with open arms and a smile. It's safe to say this rally cry is infectious, especially among the little ones." It's true—we have toddlers in our extended family who shout, "Welcome to Moe's!" every time we pass a Moe's.

If you've dined at Chick-fil-A, you know that—even when you're at the drive-thru—you'll be met with, "Good afternoon! Welcome to Chick-fil-A! How may I serve you?" That approach stands out from the mumbled greeting that we frequently hear at the typical burger joint. And instead of saying, "You're welcome," employees of Chick-fil-A will always tell you, "My pleasure!"

You might be saying, "Wait a minute, Scott—isn't this just a customer service issue?"

Yes and no. This is initially about a commitment to creativity. It's about being innovative. It's asking, "What can we do in our approach that will be imaginative, unique, and memorable?" Perhaps you come up with a slight alteration in your approach to communicating with the customer. It could be a tweak in the method of delivery of your product or service. It may be in the app your company makes available to clients.

If you really think about it, the suggestion box on the floor at a factory is just an invitation to creativity. It's asking for ideas or innovation that could improve the productivity and workflow of the plant.

Yet, I've witnessed a disdain for these kinds of efforts. In many organizations, the perception that leaders create is apparent: the managers think they know everything about plant operations—why would they ask the frontline workers for input? The home office has all the answers—why take the time to ask the cashiers in the stores for ideas?

Then, we wonder why our customers—and employees—are leaving us for the competition!

It matters less *where* you deliver a creative approach than whether or not you *do*.

Examine every point of contact you have with your customers. Where is *one* point where you can "flip the script" and deliver creatively? It only takes one.

---

3) COMMUNICATION

Never in history have we had so many tools of communication at our disposal. Change happens so fast that some people long for the "good old days" when mail (or snail mail as it's now called) and the telephone were our primary tools of communication. While every organization has some degree of proficiency when it comes to communication, those that quickly adapt to the newest forms of communication are more competitive. However, distinctive organizations and professionals take communication to a higher level in two critical aspects:

1) They communicate with their customers in the manner of the customer's choosing.
2) They use narrative as their foundation of communication.

FOLLOWING THE CUSTOMERS' LEAD

Given all the varied forms of social media—texting, FaceTime or Skype, What'sApp, Snapchat, Instagram, Facebook, email—not only do we have more ways than ever to connect, we have more opportunity to be communicating with customers in a manner they *do not* desire.

Distinctive companies will ask their customers how they wish to be contacted. If you want a text, that's what you'll get! Want a phone call? No problem. In other words, these distinctive companies aren't focused on a set policy or what's more convenient for them or the way they've always done it. They deliver their messages in the format the customer has chosen.

USE NARRATIVE IN COMMUNICATION

According to a study from the National Academy of Sciences, "People can remember more than 2,000 pictures with at least 90% accuracy in recognition tests over a period of several days, even with short presentation times during learning. This excellent memory for pictures consistently exceeds our ability to remember words."[6]

How do you transmit information to customers when they don't remember words?

You tell a story. Stories are, in essence, word pictures. They paint memorable mental images of events and create an impact in the imaginations of the listeners.

Distinctive companies are masters at narrative. They tell effective stories in which customers see themselves in a particular situation and the business as providing the solution to their problem.

To make the film *Titanic*, it cost a staggering $200 million (in 1997 dollars!). However, not many stepped out of the theater marveling over the fact that a special Russian submarine was used or that every detail on the ship matched the original Titanic down to the doorknobs. The audience walked away swooning over Jack and Rose's romance, saddened by the massive loss of life—or enraged that Jack's death could have been prevented had Rose just shared the door she was floating on!

The fact is people rarely remember the details—but they will remember how something made them feel. The power of a great story is the power to create emotional connectivity with customers and employees.

For example, I could simply say, "Your employees should make your customers happy."

Or I can tell you about the time that Jia Jiang decided to work on his fear of rejection by making at least one outrageous request a day. His plan was to go to a different business every day to ask for things he was certain would be refused. Then his plan was to post stories of each of these denials of service on his blog, "100 Days of Rejection Therapy."

However, on only his third day on the project, Jiang entered a Krispy Kreme in Austin, Texas, where he encountered shift leader Jackie Braun. Without her knowledge of his effort or his blog, Jiang asked Braun if Krispy Kreme would create a special order for him. His "sure to be rejected request" was that he wanted five doughnuts linked together like the Olympic rings, with each of the pastries matching the specific color and position on the logo.

And he told her he needed it in just fifteen minutes.

"I was honestly just hoping for a no and to go home," Jiang said later.

After exactly fifteen minutes, Braun emerged from the back with five interlocked doughnuts, looking much like the famed Olympic rings.

However, she wouldn't charge Jiang for his order! "It wasn't exactly what he wanted," Braun said. "To my eyes it wasn't perfect, so I didn't think I should charge him for it. It was the best I could do in the time allotted."

Why did Jackie Braun go to such extraordinary lengths? Her answer was simple: "We're here to make people happy."

Do you want your employees to become as committed to customer happiness? Do you wish your local Krispy Kreme had an employee like Jackie Braun? What do you suppose Braun's manager said about her efforts—especially since she did not charge the customer for all her work? I'll wager that you asked yourself at least one of those questions as you were reading the story or just after you completed it. Telling you that "employees should make customers happy" did not have a fraction of the impact that a narrative about one customer and one clerk in one donut shop delivered.

One of the stories I often tell during my speeches is of an extraordinary cab driver—Taxi Terry—from Jacksonville, Florida. (This story formed the basis of my book, *7 Tenets of Taxi Terry*.) When I tell the example of this taxi driver from the stage, practically no member of the audience is visualizing *me* in the back of the cab. Each person is seeing *herself* sitting there. When customers personalize the visualization, it has become memorable.

Many leaders have no problem retelling well-known stories about Steve Jobs, Southwest Airlines, or some other anecdote their customers or employees have read or heard. However, they frequently won't tell the stories of their own organizations. Why?

We run from our own uniqueness.

For some strange reason, we love to hear and tell the stories of others—but many have significant challenge in being able to recognize and relate their own. It's as if we have a huge blind spot regarding our own distinction.

And, by the way, if your first reaction to that statement was, "The difference is that we don't have a good story to tell," you've just confirmed your blind spot. There is a compelling story within each person and every organization.

If you find yourself with that dilemma, reach out for coaching—and there are many such consultants available. For example, Doug Stevenson (storytelling-in-business.com) teaches salespeople how to tell better stories via a method he calls Aikido Selling. According to his website, "In the ancient martial art called Aikido, you use your opponent's energy and momentum to defeat them without doing harm. In Doug's unique sales approach, the salesperson welcomes resistance, questions, and objections because they know they are prepared to embrace the objection and answer it with the appropriate story."

Larry Winget (LarryWinget.com) is a close friend I mention several times in this book. In addition to his highly successful career as a speaker and author, he consults with a limited number of executives and entrepreneurs to improve and enhance their storytelling abilities.

And this is an area in which I've helped executives with coaching and consulting. My experience has been that most of us have been well trained in data and analytics—and poorly educated in creating compelling narrative that advances our causes and careers.

Just as an editor can notice mistakes in a manuscript that have eluded the author—just as the manager can improve the swing of the famous hitter in baseball—having a professional assist you in crafting and delivering your narrative can help you see the proverbial forest amid all the trees.

By the way, that is not a solution exclusively available for corporations with big budgets for public relations. I promise there is a community college literature professor—or even a local high school English teacher—who would love to help you craft your compelling narrative. You're not asking for expertise in creating marketing copy—that's not in their wheelhouse. You are requesting their insights on your narrative, just as they would grade and improve a student's essay.

Create a compelling narrative—then start sharing it with customers and employees. The story you keep to yourself has the same value in the market as not having a story at all.

---

4) CUSTOMER EXPERIENCE

Distinctive organizations and leaders have an obsession for sensation. They are consumed with the question "What does it *feel like* to do business with us?"

Leaders who believe they can cut their way to success are fascinating to me. You've seen this play out repeatedly when an organization finds itself in difficulty. The immediate response from the leader may be to terminate senior staffers—meaning customers now can't find anyone who knows what they're doing to serve them. Maybe they scrimp a bit on maintenance—so now customers face dirty stores that are poorly stocked.

When I was growing up, my dad owned a small grocery store. He faced some tough competition when a new, larger store opened in town with greater selection and longer hours of operation. In response, my father didn't cut our staff or their pay. He did the opposite. He reduced the number of hours our store was open, increased the number of people working at the times you could shop with us, and intensified the customer experience. We would offer to carry your purchase to your car—even if you only bought a pack of gum!

While the competition was a supermarket, our store became known as the "super service market." Although I am certainly not an objective observer, the experience of shopping at that little store was beyond compare. It's why our grocery survived the impact of "big box" competition—the supermarket eventually closed its doors and left town. And it's why, with the new owners who followed when my dad retired, that little store in Crothersville, Indiana, still thrives today.

Take a moment to think about your own business. Would *you* do business with you?

Ask yourself if the experience you offer is so compelling that you would become a loyal customer. Obviously, customers want to repeat and refer extraordinary experiences.

> *It's important to note that these Cornerstones—even this final one—are for every business of every type.*

For many, it's easier to think about customer service in a retail setting. However, even companies that support other businesses—freight companies, ad agencies, accounting service providers, data repositories, law firms, and the like need to focus on their delivery of the customer experience as well. Unfortunately, some of these business-to-business (B2B) organizations assume that an intensive approach to customer relationships is only for companies selling directly to consumers. Nothing could be further from the truth!

"Today's B2B buyers bring their B2C [business to consumer] digital commerce expectations for functionality, personalization, and service to B2B eCommerce," says a recent study from Forrester Research conducted for Accenture Interactive and SAP Hybris. "Buyers want more personalization across all stages of the customer journey," the study continues, "and they're willing to reward the businesses that offer it to them. *If you don't deliver that B2C-like personalized experience, someone else will.*"[7]

For many years, I've discussed the Ultimate Customer Experience (so much so that I trademarked the term). Here is a list of steps to help you create an Ultimate Customer Experience—regardless of whether you're B2B or B2C:

1. What if *everything* went *exactly* right? Write a list of what would occur if everything—from the first point of contact to the close of the transaction—went perfectly from the customer's point of view.

2. What does it take to make it work out this way? Next, determine what you need to do—the specific action steps required—to enable the result as outlined in Step 1.

3. What are the roadblocks preventing execution? Consider any old policies or procedures that are getting in the way of delivering the Ultimate Customer Experience. Could the way it's always been done be preventing outstanding service? Whatever is delaying the delivery of the Ultimate Customer Experience—*fix it!*

4. Are we providing the tools required to deliver an Ultimate Customer Experience? Make sure your frontline people have been educated and

trained sufficiently. Do they have the tools—
physical and technological—to deliver an ultimate experience?

Your goal should be to create the Ultimate
Customer Experience for every customer—
every time!

From Distinction to Iconic!

As mentioned previously, you cannot rise to the level of
iconic status without first creating distinction. Developing an extraordinarily high level of Clarity, Creativity,
Communication, and Customer Experience can take you
to the top of the particular market that you serve. Some
organizations and leaders, however, have transcended
their specific industry to become recognized as iconic.

*What did they do above and beyond the
four cornerstones to advance beyond
distinction?*

That is the question that we will explore in the next
chapters of this book.

ICONIC

QUESTIONS FOR CHAPTER 2

- What is your organization's high-concept statement? What's your personal high-concept statement?
- Select a specific point of contact you have with a customer. What's one aspect you could approach in a more innovative manner?
- Craft a story about how doing business with you has impacted a customer—whether another business or an individual. Tell the story from the customer's point of view. (To make the story memorable to other customers and prospects, it must be about the customer—not you!)
- How would you assess the experience that customers currently receive from you? Is it systemic to your organizational culture, or is it random and dependent upon which employee they encounter? (It cannot be "ultimate" if it is random!)

PART TWO

FIVE FACTORS OF ICONIC PERFORMANCE

CHAPTER THREE

#1 Play Offense

When I hear the expression "Take it to the limit," I immediately hear the Eagles' hit song featuring Randy Meisner's soaring vocals playing in my head. It may be a cliché, but iconic companies and leaders do take it to the limit. They attain the highest level of distinction.

In my research, interviews, and observations, I've learned that there are five factors of iconic performance—those aspects that take an organization or leader to a level beyond distinction:

1. Play Offense
2. Get Promise and Performance Right
3. Stop Selling
4. Go Negative
5. Reciprocal Respect

We don't imagine that Amazon is inhibited about their plans for the future and their speed of execution. It's difficult to envision Elon Musk instructing colleagues to "take it easy"—to use another Eagles analogy—as they're executing a project. Iconic companies and leaders are widely recognized for being the ones who are constantly on the offensive.

Iconic performers concentrate
on playing offense.

In today's business, you may hear phrases such as "We are knocking it out of the park" or "Today's performance was a grand slam." While sports metaphors potentially can cause confusion with certain clients, it does help to illustrate the point that iconic leaders are aggressive in their thinking—they want to win. In my study of organizations, the phrase "We stay on offense"—or the variation "We don't focus on defense"—is repeated with great frequency. For that reason, it's what we'll use here.

In September 2015, I gave a talk on distinction in Cancun, Mexico, to all the general managers of Fairmont Hotels & Resorts. A short time after that conference, I was booked at the Fairmont Scottsdale Princess in Scottsdale, Arizona, at an unrelated event for a different company. When the team at the Princess learned I was coming as a guest, they decided to prove to me they took my material on distinction very seriously—and delivered an Ultimate Customer Experience. The director of operations, Gerard Mauvis, arranged an incredible welcome. He placed me in a magnificent suite and arranged for my rental car to be a Ferrari. (Yes, he was making a *phenomenal* impression—one that reminded me I was a long way from that small grocery in Crothersville, Indiana.)

Gerard told me he planned to develop reading groups throughout the Princess to discuss my book *What Customers REALLY Want*. Each department would read a chapter a week, then discuss how the content could be applied to housekeeping, valet parking, and every other position. He wanted to then repeat the process with *Create Distinction* to discover distinctive ways for every professional there to do their jobs. (I *loved* that idea—distinctive housekeeping, distinctive bartenders, distinctive valets.)

When I returned to visit the Fairmont Scottsdale Princess several months later, Mauvis asked a question that stopped me in my tracks.

"What's *next*, Scott?" he inquired. "What comes *after* you achieve distinction?"

Gerard Mauvis's question got me thinking—what *does* come next? I had focused on how to create distinction—but not how to maintain it, grow it, and expand beyond it. "Next you will become iconic!" I blurted out.

He smiled a broad smile. "*Yes!*" he responded. "We will become *iconic!*"

Gerard introduced me to Jack Miller, the general manager of the Scottsdale Princess—now also regional vice president of Fairmont Hotels & Resorts. Miller is a legend in the hospitality industry. In 2016, he was named the Outstanding General Manager of Large Properties in the nation by the American Hotel & Lodging Association.

Over breakfast one morning, Miller and Mauvis told me they were frustrated that a local competitor was imitating the innovations that made the Princess distinctive.

"It almost makes you want to stop innovating," Miller said. "We work so hard to create something special and unique—and they step in and rip us off."

As the discussion continued, we concluded that if the Princess ceased to innovate, it was certain the competition would catch up with them. Miller knew he had to continue innovating, he had to stay on the offensive if he was going to establish the Princess as an iconic hotel.

"I see now that every moment I spent being upset at the imitation we were seeing from the competition was a moment wasted that could have been invested in innovating to take our business to the iconic level," Miller told me later.

Every moment you are playing defense against the competition wastes a moment you could be innovating to make them irrelevant.

Choosing to be on the offense—rather than defense—means you have decided to be the initiator of action. You have resolved that you will not be as reactive to events outside your control. Primarily, it means you are exercising your power of choice regardless what others may be doing.

Besides, as Comcast CEO Neil Smit says, "It's a lot more fun than defense. It's a way of life. You get more externally focused when you play offense."[8]

When you focus on offense, you choose to spend the vast majority of your time and effort—probably at least 75 percent—planning and progressing down your desired path without any regard for what others in your industry are doing.

When the executives at ABC determine their programming schedule for the next season, they probably make their decisions based on what the other major networks—NBC, CBS, and FOX—are planning. Netflix, on the other hand, likely considers only what their customers are watching. They refuse to be bound by the traditional seasonal scheduling format and make their determinations based on customer preference instead of the competition.

Think Netflix is worried about the networks? I don't. I don't even believe they're too concerned with Hulu, Amazon, or Apple. They have taken the offensive and are charting their own course. Netflix is iconic.

While Netflix doesn't focus on Amazon, the reverse is equally true. Amazon founder Jeff Bezos has often said, "Our number one conviction and idea and philosophy and principle... is *customer* obsession, as opposed to *competitor* obsession."[9]

Notice a pattern here?

Six Steps to an Offensive Mindset

It is important to note that iconic businesses or leaders understand that playing offense is a strategy of growth and innovation. Unfortunately, some marketing consultants have an alternative approach to this point. We are all aware of marketing organizations—particularly those focused on politics—that view offensive marketing strategies as "full frontal attacks." They even engage in character assassinations and assail their competition's strengths in an attempt to twist them as weaknesses. Some of the specific strategies include:

- *flank attacks*—named for attacking weak spots of competitors
- *guerilla attacks*—subversive "hit and run" attacks to undermine your competitor
- *bypass attacks*—leapfrogging the competition through introduction of new products or services

These tactics may work, but the strategy behind it is too small. To be an iconic business, you must think much bigger—long-term. Instead of this combative type of marketing approach, your innovative thinking needs to be what Smit called "a way of life." It's both an organizational commitment and a total mindset makeover by the leadership.

Many years ago, entrepreneur and former congressman Ed Foreman related the story of the time he turned the financial results of his several companies over to his accountant. Noting the strong expansion in each sector of Foreman's diverse organization, the CPA shook his head and said, "Ed, this growth is amazing. Haven't you heard about the recession?"

Foreman responded, "Yes, but we decided not to participate."

Foreman set his own rules. Choosing how you will play the game is essential to delivering the results and building an iconic organization. It creates the kind of business that Jack Miller has generated at the Fairmont Princess and builds the type of organization that Neil Smit has at Comcast Cable. You do not have to participate in the games that competitors are playing.

Let's look at the six steps to taking the Iconic offensive mindset.

1) Choose the Game You Will Play

One of the most profound statements I heard about becoming an iconic company was from Gerard Mauvis during our initial discussions. He said: "We realized we couldn't become globally iconic until we were locally distinctive."

Remember, you must create distinction before you can achieve the iconic level. The Fairmont Scottsdale Princess exemplifies that approach. They chose the game they would play, created amazing distinction at the local level, then rode their success to iconic recognition.

Imagine you are managing a hotel in Scottsdale, Arizona. What do you think the slowest times of the year might be? You'd naturally think of the summer months—it's probably difficult to fill your resort when the temperature is 120 degrees. Another time that might be tough for you is around the Christmas holiday. There are no conventions held then and business travel drops to zero. Few families view that time of year as one to spend in a resort hotel. In addition, Arizona is home to many transplants who want to return to the East Coast or Midwest to spend Christmas with their families back home. (There's a reason Bing Crosby never sang about dreaming of a cactus and sand-filled Christmas "like the ones I used to know.")

How do you pack your hotel with guests during the time of year that the fewest number of people want to travel to your location?

Combining the ideas of the offensive mindset—choosing the game you will play and becoming locally distinctive—Jack Miller and team made a critical decision. "We decided," Miller said, "that we were going to *own* Christmas in Scottsdale."

That meant at least three things to Miller and his colleagues:

1. We will create a local tradition for the entire community.
2. What we do will be so spectacular that it will inspire repeat and referral visits.
3. It will grow our local reputation to the point that we are considered *the* distinctive property in our community.

No one else in the community was playing that game. In fact, some properties were reducing their number of employees working over the holiday and providing a lower level of service because of the sparse business. Miller, Mauvis, and their team committed to playing the game that they had chosen in a very unique manner. They created a winter wonderland with a desert ice skating rink, a build-a-toy workshop, millions of lights and light shows, a s'mores land complete with a campfire, carousel, and Ferris wheel, and much more.

The Fairmont Princess did not submit to certain "rules of engagement" and pack up for the winter because it is just the way "it's always been done." That's the essence of not selecting the game you're playing.

Don't get me wrong. I realize that for many of us, we're not going to have total control over the rules of the game. If you're a financial advisor, you must adhere to governmental and industry regulations. If you're an architect, there are certain rules of physics that will always take precedence. Even if you're the general manager of the Scottsdale Princess, you will still have to rent rooms to guests. I'm certain you already know in today's fast-changing environment that doing business as it's always been done is not going to cut it. The question is what will you *do* about it?

Tesla didn't say, "Automobiles are only sold through independent dealerships." Instead, Elon Musk and team took the offensive and decided how they would play the game. You can only buy a Tesla through Tesla show-rooms—which are usually in shopping malls, not in sub-urban "auto malls"—or online. Tesla followed the Apple model of selling products direct to consumers. In the early days, Apple didn't say, "Most computers are sold to companies through highly organized corporate sales teams." Instead, Steve Jobs and associates decided on a different field of play. Both of these companies are examples that you can make how your product is sold as distinctive as the product that you sell.

You can choose—and change—the game in every organization and at every level. A payroll department in a large organization decided to do exactly that. Instead of just "cutting payroll checks," they decided to reframe the game. They changed their motto to "We deposit the money that funds the dreams of 5,000 families— including our own."

The department leaders then started sharing the stories of the fulfilled dreams. They told their colleagues of employees who had saved to buy a boat or pay for a college education from the money the payroll team had deposited in their accounts. The results were higher productivity, lower turnover, and significantly greater job satisfaction in that department. This department is now both distinctive within the organization and iconic as a payroll team across many industries.

They decided to play a different game.

What game are you choosing? Or are you even choosing? Are you just going along for the ride—just mindlessly playing the same old game—and wondering why you aren't standing out from the competition and winning the contest?

2) DEVELOP AN INNOVATIVE GAME PLAN

At the core, our game plan is both the overall strategy for success and the specific tactics we will execute to win.

Remember the Fairmont Scottsdale Princess. The manager decided the game was to be locally distinctive and that would start with "owning" Christmas in their hometown. The next step was to deliver the tactics to accomplish that strategy.

Similar to the strategy of McDonald's with its Happy Meals and playgrounds, the team at the Princess realized that if they would appeal to kids, the parents would naturally come along. Hotels tend to market to business travelers—resorts often focus upon meetings, couples, and families. The Princess developed an aspect of their unique Christmas program that would focus on kids. (After all, parents love to give their kids memorable experiences.) If the Princess could wow the family, they would get the repeat and referral business they desired.

How would you develop such a plan? For Jack Miller and his team, it started with outlining the traditions that make Christmas special. Some were obvious—Santa Claus and Christmas lights—others took a bit more creativity given their Southwestern setting—ice skating in the desert and roasting marshmallows around a campfire. The Princess team set up a "Santa's Secret Headquarters" where kids could write a letter to Santa. Next, youngsters walk through a hallway of snow-covered trees to place their message to St. Nick in an oversized mailbox.

The Princess didn't slow down for the winter like the competition. Instead, it decided the game it wanted to play and developed strategy to play that game—and become the best at it. At no point in the process did the Princess team ask what any other resort in the area was doing. They didn't wonder, "What does the Phoenician serve for Christmas brunch?" Or "How many lights does the Four Seasons string up?"

You cannot create an innovative game plan if all you do is focus on what everyone else is delivering in your marketplace. Naturally, you have awareness of your competition. However, when you choose to play the game your way, what the opponent is doing is never a primary aspect in your game plan.

The week before Super Bowl LII, a story in *Sports Illustrated* featured the planning process that Philadelphia Eagles coach Doug Pederson employed in the attempt to win against an iconic competitor. "In the pregame mayhem this week," famed reporter Peter King wrote, "there is sure to be this story line: *Belichick vs. Pederson: Mismatch of Super Bowl 52.* Pederson gets it. He was a Louisiana high school coach ten years ago when Belichick already had three Super Bowl rings."

(The Patriots are the NFL's reigning dynasty and Patriots coach Bill Belichick is recognized by most football experts as one of the—if not *the*—greatest coach in the history of the NFL.) Coach Pederson was asked how many times he had mentioned the Patriots or Belichick to his team of coaches or the players.

"Zero," Pederson said. "I have not."

Pederson called his strategy the "faceless opponent."

"I just think you can't get caught up with who's on the other side," he said. "Everybody in the NFL is good. Every team is good. I've always believed you just go about your business. You prepare. You get your team ready to go every week, and you treat it that way. It's about doing your job. That fits with the faceless opponent. Do what you've been coached to do this week. . . win your matchup, the one-on-ones, and let's see what happens. *Nothing else matters, so why introduce anything else?*"[10]

When you decide to approach the marketplace with an offensive mindset, it strengthens the likelihood that you can create an innovative game plan.

3) PLAY TO YOUR STRENGTHS

A team of researchers wrote a great piece published in the *Harvard Business Review* on managers playing to their strengths. It is the best way to reach your highest potential. "After all, it's a rare baseball player who is equally good at every position. Why should a natural third baseman labor to develop his skills as a right fielder?"[11]

A fundamental element of playing offense is to play to the strengths of your organization and the people on your team.

You likely know the result of the Super Bowl LII. The underdog Eagles "beat the (New England Patriots) Belichick-Brady conglomerate—the greatest coach/quarterback duo in the game's history—and he did it with a backup quarterback [Nick Foles] who nearly retired in 2015 because he questioned whether he had enough enthusiasm left to continue playing."[12]

"'We just wanted to stay aggressive,' Pederson said afterward. 'My mentality coming into the game was to stay aggressive until the end and let playmakers make plays,' Pederson said."[13]

The Fairmont Scottsdale Princess believed they had advantages in the areas of both property and people. The goal became to play to their strengths.

The physical facility was a critical aspect that would permit them to create a memorable experience. The resort is on sixty-five acres in the heart of the Sonoran Desert next to the McDowell Mountains. The sheer size of the property was a strength that allowed the team to create special areas within the resort for the Christmas project—such as a six-thousand-square-foot ice skating rink (with real ice in the middle of the desert) and a giant four-story Christmas tree with seventy thousand LED lights and a five-foot snowflake tree topper.

Yet, Miller and Mauvis constantly reminded me that it was the team of professionals at the Princess who made it all happen. They believed in their staff that included industry "playmakers"—and they were called on to make some big plays.

"Our people are our greatest asset" is a phrase we've heard leaders exclaim time and time again. However, many recite this line while simultaneously treating their employees as nothing more than an expense. So what's your initial, gut-level reaction to this question: are your employees *primarily* an asset or an expense to your business?

Many leaders claim their people are their greatest asset but then go on to treat them as nothing more than an expense. Consider this report from CityLab in 2013:

> The average American cashier makes $20,230 a year, which in a single-earner household would leave a family of four living under the poverty line. But if he works the cash registers at QuikTrip, it's an entirely different story. The convenience store and gas station chain offers entry-level employees an annual salary of around $40,000, plus benefits. Those high wages didn't stop QuikTrip from prospering in a hostile economic climate. While other low-cost retailers spent the recession laying off staff and shuttering stores, QuikTrip expanded to its current 645 locations across 11 states.[14]

If you see your people primarily as an expense, you naturally will seek to minimize them.

If you see your people primarily as an expense, that expenditure becomes an aspect of your business that you typically seek to minimize. In other words, we're taught in business that profit is enhanced—at least in part—by reducing expenses. The more we keep our expenses in check, this basic theory of business goes, the greater the likelihood we will become more profitable.

That's not the *total* picture, though. Assets are vital points in our business that we seek to amplify. When we go on the offensive, we seek to make our assets more valuable. When you see your employees as assets to be cultivated and enhanced—as opposed to expenses to reduce and minimize—those assets become more productive—and, therefore, more profitable—for your business.

CityLab found that "entry-level hires at QuikTrip are trained for two full weeks before they start work, and they learn everything from how to order merchandise to how to clean the bathroom."

Why is that important? "As global competition increases and cheap, convenient commerce finds a natural home online, the most successful companies may be those that *focus on delivering a better customer experience*."[15]

That experience is delivered by your "playmakers."

> *To attain iconic status, you must seek to enhance and play to the strengths of your team.*

The *Harvard Business Review* report states, "It is a paradox of human psychology that while people remember criticism, they respond to praise. The former makes them defensive and therefore unlikely to change, while the latter produces confidence and the desire to perform better."[16] When it comes to praise and playing to the strengths of the team, I don't know that I have met any leader who is as relentlessly positive as Jack Miller at the Scottsdale Princess.

- Imagine working for someone who sees you as an asset, has confidence in you, and gives you the tools to succeed.
- Visualize a coach who tries to take pressure off you by not harping on the competition.
- Consider what it would be like to be an employee under a leader whose core principle is to play to the strengths of her team members.

Do you suppose that type of commitment and trust would inspire greater performance, engagement, and loyalty with your team?

It's not a coincidence that QuikTrip paid its cashiers almost *double* the industry standard and simultaneously grew the business. It's not merely by chance that the *Forbes*, Glassdoor, and LinkedIn lists of Best Places to Work constantly feature iconic companies like Salesforce, Wegman's, In-N-Out Burger, Google, Lululemon, and SAP. We'll explore the iconic corporate culture later, in chapter seven of this book.

When you play to your strengths—
recognizing your strength is in your
people and how you help them develop—
you can take an offensive position in the
marketplace.

4) Capture Attention

Ben Parr is a journalist, author, and venture capitalist. When we were both speaking at the Brand Manage Camp in 2017, he talked about capturing people's attention.

> Your long-term success depends on winning the attention of others. If your boss doesn't notice your work, how will you get a promotion? If your team doesn't listen to you, how can you lead effectively? And if you can't capture the attention of clients, how does your business or career survive? . . .

The most effective employees, managers, and executives are the ones who shine a spotlight on their ideas, projects, and teams. Understanding the science of attention is a prerequisite to success in the information age.[17]

In the case of the Scottsdale Princess, three million dazzling LED lights, an animated holiday light show, a large Ferris wheel, a Christmas carousel, and an ice slide are among the innovative elements that capture the attention of the entire Phoenix metropolitan area and beyond.

In the age of the Internet and social media and blogging, attention spans are shorter than ever. You must ask the question: what are we doing to capture the interest of our audience?

> To take the offensive, you cannot major in
> minor projects.

---

5) HOLD THE PLAYERS ACCOUNTABLE

The late Pat Summitt, legendary Tennessee women's basketball coach, said, "Responsibility equals accountability equals ownership. And a sense of ownership is the most powerful weapon a team or organization can have."

Coaches of top athletes and management experts agree that an essential component to staying on the offensive is to hold the players on your team accountable for their actions and results. According to Gordon Tredgold, business coach and consultant, there are three purposes for this:

1. It lets them know that they will be held accountable for the activities.
2. It gives you an opportunity to provide support in case things start to go awry.

3. It offers you the opportunity to offer praise and encouragement to move people further if things are going well.[18]

Could you imagine the coach allowing a player who was performing badly—or not caring about the outcome of the game—to continue to play in the game? While that's unheard of in athletics, it is often the case in business. For some reason, there are many who seldom choose to call out a colleague when their attitude is below par. It seems in today's sensitive and litigious world, managers are afraid to upset or offend. The problem is that by failing to hold their team members accountable, they frequently upset and offend those who *are* performing at the levels we expect and desire.

Peter Bregman is renowned author and leadership coach. Bregman began his career teaching leadership on wilderness and mountaineering expeditions, then moved into the consulting field. Since 1989, he has trained and coached all levels of management. He teaches that there are five clear ways to hold people accountable:

1. **Clear expectations**: be precise about what you expect in terms of performance and outcomes.
2. **Clear capabilities**: be exact about what's needed to get the job done—and whether that individual team member has the capacity to achieve it.

3. **Clear measurement**: be open about how the performance will be evaluated—and what constitutes success or failure.

4. **Clear feedback**: open, honest, and transparent reviews throughout the process are required to keep everyone on track.

5. **Clear consequences**: be certain there's no ambiguity on what will happen when performance is delivered—or the team member fails to achieve success. [19]

French philosopher and playwright Moliere once wrote, "It is not only what we do, but also what we do *not* do, for which we are accountable."

You cannot develop iconic performance
without accountability.

You'll never stimulate a culture that's
constantly on the offense if you fail to hold
your players to a high standard.

---

6) CELEBRATE THE VICTORIES

When I entered my room during a recent visit to the Fairmont Scottsdale Princess, a video was playing on the flat-screen television. At first glance, it appeared to be the performance of a circus. On closer examination, I noticed that the ringmaster was none other than Jack Miller and many of those in the audience were members of the Princess team I had grown to know over the past few years.

To celebrate their becoming an iconic hotel and resort, the leadership team had thrown a private circus performance for the entire resort staff and their families. It was the leadership's way of congratulating the employees on a job well done—and served as another reminder of the family-oriented culture that Miller and his colleagues work to ingrain throughout the organization.

When you decide to celebrate a success:

1. Don't wait
2. Make it special
3. Deliver a tangible

DON'T WAIT

Picture an NFL game where the official says to the players, "You have to wait until halftime to dance in the end zone for the scores you have accumulated over the previous two quarters of football." Are you kidding?

Could you even imagine an announcer prior to a basketball game warning the fans, "To enhance the concentration of our players, do not cheer after each basket—please wait until the designated breaks to display enthusiasm for your team." Obviously not!

Players dance and fans cheer *immediately* when their player scores or makes a big play. It's a visceral reaction. We have to cheer.

So why do we frequently take a different approach in business? Why do we wait to schedule a meeting to read a list of accomplishments from the past several weeks—or even months? That's a poor approach to recognition.

When someone has done something deserving of recognition, don't wait. You may debate the appropriateness of instant expressions of commendation. However, in this day and age, it is a proven and effective leadership tool.

Make it special

I have been at conferences where awards for exceptional performance were being presented and the chief executive officer has commented, "This is the most important—and enjoyable—part of my position as CEO of this company." I *love* hearing that!

One idea is to reconsider the names that you assign to the awards and recognition.

For example, being named a customer service *superstar* is infinitely more special than receiving an award for fewest customer complaints. (I've actually seen both of those awards presented to exceptional employees!) I swooned when a CEO presented a receptionist with an award titled Hero of First Impressions—instead of handing a gift and unemotionally thanking her for her service to the company. Review how you recognize achievement and find ways to enhance the level of excitement it creates for your team. Be creative and distinctive even in this area.

Deliver a tangible

Jack Miller not only is ringmaster of a circus to reward his team, he is a master at handwritten notes of appreciation. Miller understands that customer and employee experience is critical. He makes sure to "leave behind a trail of tangibles," as my close friend and president of High Point University Dr. Nido Qubein suggests.

In other words:

- Don't just send an email to give a high performer a day off. Hand-deliver a printed "day-off pass" to them and personally thank them.
- Do not simply buy a meal at a nice restaurant. Arrange to have the menu signed by the chef and framed as a keepsake of a special occasion.

The point is to go above and beyond not just in the way you reach customers but the way you treat employees too. They "respond to appreciation expressed through recognition of their good work because it confirms their work is valued by others," writes consultant Kim Harrison.[20]

Our job is to deliver tangible recognition in a manner that keeps our teammates delivering and on the offensive.

THE IMPORTANCE OF PLAYING OFFENSE

"Defense wins championships," goes the old saying.

Except it isn't true. The better defense does not win even half of the time.

Consider this: thirty-eight Super Bowl winners had a top-ten *offense.*

According to an analysis on Freakonomics.com, "There have been 427 NFL playoff games over the last 45 seasons. The better defensive teams have won 58 percent of them. The better offensive teams have won 62 percent of the time."[21] (The winning team sometimes is better on both sides of the ball, explaining why the total exceeds 100 percent.)

Maybe I'm a bit prejudiced when it comes to this statistic because my favorite NFL team, the Indianapolis Colts, won Super Bowl XLI with a team rated nineteenth in the league on defense—but *third on offense.*

It's interesting to me that when the NFL, NHL, NBA, or MLB presents their respective Most Valuable Player awards, it is almost always for the player who has had the best season in terms of offensive statistics. Many of those leagues even have a best defensive player award to recognize a player's excellence on that side of the ball or puck. Yet, "most valuable" is, in many cases, the best *offensive* player.

In other words, the best *offensive* efforts are the ones considered as the most valuable to the team and the sport.

To emphasize my point: "Which of the following set of names is more recognizable? The top five touchdown leaders in NFL history: Jerry Rice, Emmitt Smith, LaDainian Tomlinson, Randy Moss, and Terrell Owens? Or the top five interception leaders: Paul Krause, Emlen Tunnell, Rod Woodson, Dick Lane, and Ken Riley?"[22]

Those of you who follow football likely remember more offensive players than defensive ones.

The same is true for iconic companies or individuals. We remember the ones who take charge and lead the offense. Remember, every moment you are playing defense against the competition wastes a moment you could be innovating to make them irrelevant.

Stop playing defense. Start now to create and deliver an innovative and dynamic offensive approach to your customers and employees.

You cannot make your competition
irrelevant while worrying about them all
the time. Play offense!

QUESTIONS FOR CHAPTER 3

- Do you feel your organization is primarily playing offense or defense? Why? If playing defense, what could you be doing to strengthen your offense?
- Are you choosing the game you play—and the way you play it—or is that dictated by external forces like the economy and the competition? If you are controlled by external forces, what can you do to be more independent of them?
- Is your game plan innovative—or do you feel as though you're just repeating traditional approaches?
- What are the strengths of your organization? What are your personal strengths? How could you play to them more of the time?
- Do you have the attention of those you need—customers, prospects, and employees?
- What do you need to do to enhance the attention you receive?
- Are people held accountable in your organization? Are you holding the people who report to you accountable for their performance? How do you enhance the level of accountability in your organization?
- Do you celebrate—quickly, publicly, and tangibly—the successes of your team members? How could you improve?

CHAPTER FOUR

#2 GET THE PROMISE AND PERFORMANCE RIGHT

You might take your car to a shop for a regularly scheduled service. Maybe you hire an IT company to manage your company's systems. Perhaps you select an advertising agency to create a campaign to tell the world about your products. It might be that you decide on a financial advisor to administer your family's resources and plan for your retirement. In every case—personal or professional—you need to ask:

- How will you evaluate the results?
- How will you determine if the decision you made was good or bad?
- How will you decide to continue the relationship—or search for another provider?

Iconic companies and leaders don't make it right—they get it right.

The research is clear: iconic companies and leaders don't *make* it right—they *get* it right. They are precise about the two primary factors that determine how we consciously—and subconsciously—evaluate them: promise and performance. These two factors are fundamental in our decisions whether we will repeat our business with them—and whether or not we will refer friends and colleagues.

The two primary factors of customer evaluation are promise and performance.

"Gallup research has shown that if customers don't have a firm foundation of confidence and trust in a brand, customer loyalty erodes," wrote William J. McEwen, author of *Married to the Brand.* "In fact," he continued, "across an array of brands in six different product categories, Gallup found that customer loyalty plummets an average of 29% if customers do not have a strong belief in the company's ability and commitment to keep its promises."[23]

Customers judge companies primarily upon how they perform relative to their promise.

Customers judge companies not only upon what they promise to do but also on how they deliver on that promise. Iconic companies are superior in the alignment of a compelling promise with consistent performance. That may sound basic and simplistic, but the more you drill down into this principle, the more complex it becomes.

> *Iconic companies are superior in the alignment of a compelling promise with consistent performance.*

A few years back, a principal business catchphrase was, "Your brand is a promise." In other words, the promise and commitment that your organization makes to customers—and employees—determines the primacy of your brand in the competitive marketplace. Often-cited examples were Safety = Volvo or Joy = Disney.

Yet, you might be asking, if your brand was simply your promise, does that mean all you have to do is make a bigger, better promise than your competitor to gain an advantage? Not exactly. An organization or leader must deliver on the promises made. Your brand is not your promise, for the promise may not be the most critical aspect in the brand equation.

As you know, Jeff Bezos is many things: founder of Amazon, owner of the *Washington Post*, and currently the world's richest person, to name a few. He also has delivered my favorite definition of what a brand *really* is: it is what people say about you when you're not in the room.

*"Your brand is what people say about
you when you're not in the room."*
—Jeff Bezos

That's perfect! Your brand is not what you promise your customers. It's what customers say about how you have performed—based on the promise to others.

- The brand of the Scottsdale Princess is what I—and other guests—tell my friends about my experience when I return home from a trip.
- The brand of my financial advisor is what I say over a cup of coffee to my wife about our advisor's performance and the experience she's created.
- Amazon's brand is, in part, how you feel about getting a delivery from them on time, even when you don't expect it—and telling all your friends. (More on that later.)

Your brand isn't just your promise.

*Your brand is how customers evaluate
the performance you have delivered
based on the promise they perceive you
have made.*

This means that we must examine both:

1. The promise we are making—and how it is perceived.
2. How our performance is stacking up against the standard that our promise implies.

PROMISE

What are you promising your customers? What should they expect when they do business with you? How about your employees—what are you promising them?

A promise, in the sense we are considering it here, is interpersonal. In other words, it is a commitment between two or more companies or two or more people. At its core, a promise is simply a commitment for action. Promises can be

- between individuals in their personal lives ("I promise to remain faithful.")
- between professionals ("I promise I'll have the report completed today.")
- between organizations ("We promise to complete the building on time and under budget.")

For over fifteen years, I've written and spoken about the importance of perception and understanding the elements of a transaction that a customer has a right to expect. Note that if I "expect you to deliver," it presumes that I perceive that a promise of some kind has been made. Why would I hold the expectation that you'll deliver something you haven't promised?

Frequently, I will ask the leadership team of an organization to list the basic elements of their product or service that any and every customer has a right to expect they deliver based on their sales pitch or promise.

The results of this exercise never cease to amaze me. In all my years of facilitating this exercise, I don't think I've ever had but a few companies—or leaders—tell me they have such a list. They usually have a list of things they don't do because of liability issues—hardly any have lists of what they always deliver for the customer. Only a small fraction has developed the list of *nonnegotiables* that a customer will always receive.

Let me explain what I mean.

I'm a Global Services-level flyer on United Airlines. Would I fly United if their motto (or stated promise) was, "We don't crash—often!" Absolutely not! Safety is a nonnegotiable; it's a given. United—and every other airline—*must* get safety right every time. If they don't, nothing else matters to their customers. Some other promises I expect from airlines include:

- The flight should be on time (if weather and other safety-related circumstances permit).
- Service should be friendly and efficient.

- The airline should deliver the promised frequent flyer rewards.
- Baggage should reach the same destination that I do—at the same time I do.
- Planes will be clean and well maintained.

You get the idea. This list should be easy to develop; however, few leaders take the time or make the effort to do it. Stop right now and create the list for your organization. In addition, make a list of what employees (your "internal customers") have a right to expect from you and your engagement with them. After you've developed your list, the next step is to ask an important question: what is the primary promise that customers believe we have made to them? You might need to:

- take a look at what your marketing efforts are suggesting;
- inquire from your sales professionals what they find most persuasive to prospective buyers;
- seek insight from your call center on what issues customers are talking about the most; and
- examine every other segment in your organization where a promise has been made or implied to customers or employees.

It's critical that you become totally clear and precise about the promise you are making. If you fail to perform, customers *will* hold you accountable. And—as many businesses, entrepreneurs, and frontline professionals already know—through social media channels, such as Yelp, Trip Advisor, Twitter, and Facebook, customers now have a bigger megaphone than ever to voice any dissatisfaction.

What happens when you feel you have delivered on the promise you have made—and customers still aren't happy? The obvious answer is that the level of "performance" you are delivering may be different from the customer's standard of expectations. We will examine that point later in this chapter. The answer that I believe is more prevalent—and much less obvious—is that you and your customer are *perceiving* the promise differently.

> *The challenge is that customers will always evaluate your performance based on the promise from their point-of-view . . . not yours.*

This is an issue that every organization and leader must confront. There is a fundamental problem with perception: customer and employee perceptions are subjective and influenced by past or comparable performances. Even iconic companies are not immune to this challenge.

We know that our promise to customers is an interpersonal commitment. But the perception of what is being promised is *intrapersonal.*

In other words, an individual will perceive a promise based on their own experiences and beliefs. Their perception is very personal and unique. If you fail to deliver based on the customer's perception, the result will be disconnection, distrust, dissatisfaction— or in the case of employees, significantly higher levels of turnover.

For example, it is my contention that the iconic company Apple is experiencing a growing gulf with their customers because of the perception problem. Apple is known for making intuitive and simple-to-use products. My first computer was the Apple IIe. Because of my lack of computer acumen, it was really nothing more than a glorified word processor for my new small business. My one significant accomplishment on it was figuring out mail merge—so I could easily address multiple envelopes and send letters that appeared to be personalized to a database of prospective clients.

When I got my new Macintosh Plus, I became a devoted fan. Every program had a similar interface and was easy to use—everything just *worked*. When Apple released the Mac SE, I was at the front of the line. It had an 8 MHz processor (my Mac Pro now has a 1600 MHz processor). I hardly knew what to do with all the computational power. It also came with 2 GB of memory, a floppy disk drive, and a hard drive with 40 MB of space for documents—less than some of my individual files today. Although it had amazing power for its time, the reason I was thrilled with it was because it was the "computer for the rest of us"—and it really was. Frankly, I don't recall ever cracking open a manual, because the Mac was so intuitive.

Fast forward to today—as I type this chapter on my MacBook Pro and I look at my iPhone X on the table beside me and the Apple Watch on my left wrist—I'm still a devoted customer of the company and am honored to have it as a client of mine. But quite frankly, my passion for them has eroded just a bit. The products aren't as simple as they once were—or as I once perceived them to be.

Now, it seems as though there is something different and unique about each program or product for the Mac that has a bit of a learning curve for the user. Certainly, Final Cut Pro is infinitely more complex than a program like Adobe PageMaker that I purchased many years ago. However, the promise of uniformity—while not absent—certainly has been ablated a bit.

The same is true with my iPhone. I became accustomed to having just one button—a tradition at Apple starting with the first iPod. Now I must learn gestures on how to swipe the screen or push the proper button in the correct sequence to get the device to do what I want it to do. With the iPhone X, I have to learn at least a dozen "intuitive" gestures that seem about as easy and natural to me as understanding the hand signals of a third-base coach. Then there are ten gestures to learn to get the basic services of the Apple Watch. That's twenty-two gestures to memorize. On the other hand, there's still just one button for my iPad.

Certainly, I realize that I'm getting very close to older generational "get off my lawn" bitching here. Yet, it's not that I'm upset about a relatively high number of gestures or methods of use of their products—it's that I feel that Apple hasn't delivered on what I perceived to be their fundamental promise: *ease of use.*

Perhaps part of this phenomenon is because our perceptions *change* based upon our performance. According to research by University of Virginia Professor Dennis Proffitt and his then-graduate student Jessica Witt, now a professor at Purdue University:

> "In their (Proffit and Witt's) experiment, 23 volunteers had to kick an American football through the field goal from the 10-yard line. After a warm-up, participants were asked to judge the height and width of the goal by adjusting a handheld, scaled-down model of the goal made out of PVC pipes. They then each performed 10 kicks. Immediately after the final kick, participants repeated the perceptual measurement.

> The result was striking. Before kicking, both groups had the same perception of the size of the goal (incidentally, an inaccurate one: everybody underestimated its actual width-to-height ratio). But after 10 kicks, the poor performers (those who scored two or fewer successful kicks)

saw the goal as about 10 percent narrower than they had before, whereas the good kickers (those who scored three or more) perceived the goal to be about 10 percent wider.

How well you have performed over the past few minutes influences the way you see the world! Not just meta-phorically, but on a physiological level—it changes your actual perceptions."[24]

Perhaps part of the problem is that your customer's perception changes as their performance with your product changes.

My perception of Apple's promise has always been "insanely great products that are easy to use." Therefore, it's likely that as Apple products have become more complex and I find them more difficult to use, my perception about the organization and how it delivers has been altered. In other words, as I'm swiping the wrong way (missing kicks, so to speak), I'm also perceiving the company is not delivering what I desire (they're making the goal posts narrower).

The more I've considered it, however, I suggest that there has been a shift at Apple's headquarters as well. CEO Tim Cook states that the "North Star" of Apple is "making insanely great products that really change the world in some way—enrich people's lives."[25]

Is it possible, though, they have come to believe that the only way they can do this is through the most advanced—and thus complex—technology achievable?

(Perhaps, too, they have their eye a bit more on the competition than they should. We all know that a new feature on the next Samsung device has a good chance of being included on a future iPhone—and vice versa.)

Please don't misunderstand me. I'm one of the 97 percent of satisfied Apple Watch customers. [26] It's just that I've moved from being "over the moon" and "thrilled" to being just "satisfied." And, while certainly not scientific, I cannot help but notice that every time I use this illustration in a speech, many members of the audience enthusiastically nod their heads in agreement.

The significant point here isn't even about Apple. It's about the fundamental importance of having a deep understanding of what your customers perceive your promise to be—because that is their benchmark for evaluation.

Apple is probably doing it exactly right, based upon what Tim Cook perceives is the proper execution of their "North Star." But what if your customers are using a sextant with a different alignment?

Here are three significant steps for achieving iconic status as it pertains to perception:

1. Clearly and precisely craft your promise to your customers.
2. Adjust and tweak your promise so it aligns with the perception of the majority of your customer base.
3. Ensure congruency between the internal and external perceptions of your promise. If your team holds one perception and your customers have a different version, it is a breeding ground for disconnection.

PERFORMANCE

How effective you are at delivering exactly what you've promised to your customers is the essence of performance. As my pal Larry Winget says, "Do what you say you will do, when you said you will do it."

"Do what you say you will do, when you said you will do it."

Many companies and professionals have difficulty executing at even this basic level. They concoct reasons—what customers call "excuses"—for why they didn't deliver as promised. However, when we do what we say we will do, customers are not only appreciative—in many cases, they want to tell the world.

A longtime friend and former coworker of mine, John T. Howard, recently posted a powerful message for his thousands of followers to read on Facebook. It was about an experience he had with an iconic company:

"Here is a precise reason why Amazon is killing traditional retail as we know it. . . .

On Friday I needed a specific lawn treatment application and went to Menards to buy it. Menards was out of stock.

I also needed a specific health supplement recommended by my cardiologist that turned out to be unavailable from local retailers. In other words, I was looking two places for two separate, completely different items. When I got home from the futile 'snipe hunt' on Friday, I found both items on Amazon for less money.

Because I am an Amazon Prime member, two-day delivery is guaranteed—including Sundays.

I forgot when I ordered that Sunday (today) is Brickyard 400 day. (*Author's note: The Brickyard 400 in Indianapolis is one of the major races on the NASCAR circuit. Even though attendance has declined in recent years, there were still about 50,000 fans crowding into the few blocks surrounding John Howard's home on this day.*)

Our usually quiet neighborhood is now crawling with cars, cops, helicopters, and people on foot—some of whom are already inebriated—who are walking in the street oblivious to traffic.

Thirty minutes ago, my 8-pound Amazon box arrived—*just as they had guaranteed!* It was delivered by a guy ON A BICYCLE with a basket.

When I asked about the bicycle, the delivery guy stated that—given the race—the packages he was delivering in the neighborhood today required something more agile than a truck.

The truck with the goodies ordered by Amazon customers in my neighborhood is parked next to Kohl's near Crawfordsville Road. Two guys with bikes are shuttling packages on race day throughout the neighborhood—so that Amazon can *keep its promise* of delivery.

I find this amazing. Amazon's success in this case seems well-deserved."[27]

It shouldn't escape us that John Howard is thrilled with Amazon not because they gave him a discount, offered an upgrade, or any of the other "underpromise, overdeliver" gimmicks that we've assumed are business gospel. Instead, he was amazed because they *did what they promised they would do.*

The Promise-Performance Matrix

The promise-performance matrix is comprised of four possible combinations that can occur in any business transaction:

1. Low promise, low performance
2. High promise, low performance
3. High promise, high performance
4. Low promise, high performance

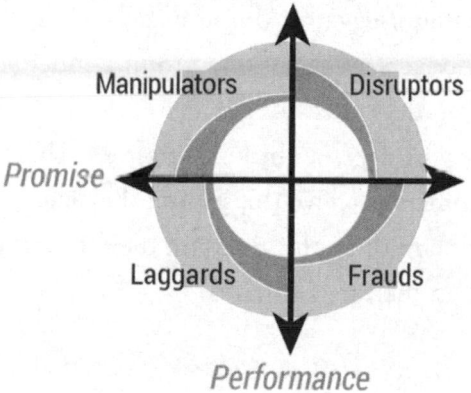

First, let's define the four styles on the matrix. Then we'll discover the "sweet spot" where iconic companies place and maintain their organizations.

Laggards (Low Promise, Low Performance)

In 1962, eminent sociologist Dr. Everett Rogers proposed the "diffusions of innovations theory" in which he developed five categories of businesses or people: innovators, early adopters, early majority, late majority, and—at the trailing end—a group consisting of approximately 16 percent of the market that Rogers designated as the laggards.

One positive comment you can make about laggards is this: they keep their word!

Certainly, laggards do not deliver much to customers. Conversely, they don't promise much, either.

The word *laggard* dates to 1757. Its original meaning was "one who lags, a shirker, loiterer." That's precisely how customers perceive this group: they lag behind their competition in their promises and they shirk the industry standards in their performance.

Laggards are low on promise and low on performance.

While Rogers first described laggards over fifty years ago as bound by tradition and conservative in approach, today's laggard is more difficult to pigeonhole. Yet we could analyze some famed national companies and categorize them as fitting into this segment.

Sears is a good example of a laggard. They offer discounts on about everything. Low prices and wide selection seems to be their promise. Yet we know that there are other retailers—Walmart comes to mind—stocking a range of anything from lawn mowers to leisure wear at lower prices. One problem is that Sears is trying to compete from higher priced real estate. When I visited a Sears store recently, I had trouble getting anyone to help me, and when I finally did get help, they weren't knowledgeable about the product.

Sears' promise is dated and old, and their performance is poor.

FRAUDS (HIGH PROMISE, LOW PERFORMANCE)

There's no kind way to put this.

If you intentionally promise what you cannot deliver, you're a fraud. Or as they say in Texas, "You're all hat and no cattle."

It has been easy to find stories in the news about companies that were fraudulent—leaders and organizations who promised customers and investors the stars but delivered nothing. I wrote specifically about one that had deceived me in a previous book.

You may be familiar with the story of Elizabeth Holmes. She was CEO of a biotech startup called Theranos that has been charged with fraud by the Securities and Exchange Commission. Holmes "once promised to revolutionize the multibillion-dollar blood testing industry with innovative finger-prick tests she said would deliver results quickly, painlessly, and cheaply."[28]

The company could verify none of those results. Their web of deceit was vast and their false promises were stunning. Holmes claimed, "The US Department of Defense was using Theranos's products on the battlefield in Afghanistan and on medevac helicopters, bringing in more than $100 million in revenue in 2014." The SEC said otherwise. Apparently Theranos' technology was never deployed by the DoD, and it generated only a little more than $100,000 in revenue in 2014. Holmes "promoted a key blood-testing product using unfounded claims." [29]

While high-profiles stories like this leave us aghast, you and I encounter smaller but similar promise-performance fraud on a regular basis:

- The waiter who promises the specials are "fantastic"—not because they are but because he's been told to push them.
- The salesperson who assures you that customers "love our product"— not because they really do but to make the sale.
- The business owner who tells the creative professional how much he "values her work"—then rips off her ideas so he doesn't have to pay for her concepts.

There was a service provider I did business with regularly because I liked the charismatic owner a lot. I considered the owner to be a personal friend and a good guy. When we were having difficulty with their product, though, his response was always, "Just wait until you see our next version—it will knock you out!" I'm not proud to admit how long I continued to do business with them, but he finally crossed the line. Make no mistake, there is always a line in the sand for every customer.

Because of the shortsighted approach of the frauds, they seldom recognize that those customers who finally see through their con game will not only stop doing business with them—some will make it their mission to do what it takes to help drive other customers away.

- If you are dealing with a fraudulent business, stop immediately. It will only get worse.
- If you read this and feel a little pang of guilt for some fraudulent claim you made, stop immediately. Make a list of the promises you've made to your customers and employees. Attempt to repair the damage of your falsehoods before you make any additional promises.

DISRUPTORS (HIGH PROMISE, HIGH PERFORMANCE)

Disruptors begin at a point of pain and dissatisfaction with the options currently available and work tirelessly to make high promises and overdeliver.

> *The genesis of all disruption is dissatisfaction.*

No one truly liked standing on a street corner in the rain, waving frantically at passing yellow vehicles, desperately hoping that one would decide to favor you with a pickup. Entering the cab, you might be met by a surly driver you could barely understand and with an odor you could barely endure. You wondered throughout your experience if he was taking the most direct path to your destination or taking advantage of you. By the time you exited, you may have been happy to simply depart with your luggage and your health.

Uber and Lyft changed all of that. From your smartphone, you merely indicate where you want to be driven. Almost instantly, you receive information about your ride—complete with a picture of the driver, the type of car she is driving, and her license plate number. You can track the ride on your device—both to view the arrival of your car and to ensure you're taking the right route during your trip—and it's totally cashless. The ride is instantly billed to your credit card, and you tip the driver on the app.

Uber and Lyft made their promises big—they were highly innovative and disruptive. Yet it goes beyond that. They *performed* on their promises. It just works. That is what has enabled Uber and Lyft to become disruptors and iconic companies.

Certainly, there have been challenges that Uber has faced as an organization—many because of the boorish behavior of founder and former CEO, Travis Kalanick.

Kalanick's conduct reportedly included rude comments to employees, leadership that was certainly sophomoric for a CEO and perhaps misogynistic, and a displayed disregard for the rules ranging from violation of app guidelines and restrictions by Apple to accusations by Google of stealing trade secrets. [30]

Yet most of us kept on using the Uber app. The reason is promise/performance. Their big promise was still compelling, and the performance we personally received as a customer was delivered in a manner that was congruent. While the CEO was saying and doing reprehensible things, the organization was doing what they said they would do for customers—at the Disruptor level.

This is not to suggest that I believe we should ignore reprehensible behavior from corporate executives. We *shouldn't*. The reason to mention this situation is that simple observation confirms the average customer was able to put aside the lack of congruency from one executive so as not punish many hardworking drivers for a single individual's behavior—an issue over which the drivers had no control. The Uber Board of Directors did what was required to get bad behavior out of the corporate suite, just as we appreciated the promise/performance execution of the larger team of about 12,000 employees and 160,000 independent contractor drivers.

Disruptors understand that the customer's perception of their promise is high—in part because it goes against the bland, standard approach that consumers have grown to find dissatisfactory. Therefore, when an organization can deliver on a new kind of promise, customers naturally assume that your high benchmark of performance will make a powerful impact on the marketplace.

When Professor Jeff Wilson said he wanted to change housing, he proved that he meant it. Wilson wanted to learn more about the limits of how much space we need as human beings. So he decided to put himself to the test.

Wilson made a thirty-three-square-foot dumpster his home for a year. "While the experiment was extreme, the experience he gained by living small and simple made a big impression," his company's website states. "At the end of the year, he left the dumpster with the concept for a new category of housing — a beautiful, small footprint home designed as a solution for the growing housing crisis."[31]

Wilson formed Kasita in 2015, which now manufacturers 374-square-foot micro-homes that can be anything from a guesthouse, cabin in the country, unit for a rental home on your existing property, or just about anything else you could imagine. Features on these micro-homes can be upgraded to include exclusive Bosch appliances, Casper mattresses, and Sonos sound throughout.

The units are even stackable—meaning they could become apartment communities, condo groups, or home/office units.

Wilson and his team in Austin, Texas, have made an interesting and aggressive promise. The marketplace will determine if their performance throughout the range of services they need to provide—including quality manufacturing, safe delivery, financing, assistance with zoning regulations, and more—will move Kasita to the level of an iconic disruptor. (The future looks good for them. *Inc.* named Kasita as one of the 25 Most Disruptive Companies of the Year in 2017.)[32]

Why does the type of disruption we've talked about here—from Uber to Kasita—seem to happen through start-ups instead of established companies?

It's partly because of the phenomenon Dr. Clayton Christenson describes in his 2013 book *The Innovator's Dilemma*. Companies tend to seek to improve existing products incrementally to protect their franchise. Start-ups aren't burdened with economic and emotional loyalty to past products or way of doing things. They are free to raise the standard.

Another facet is that start-ups are nimbler. After a while, the high promises that have been made by disruptors lose their luster and are no longer valued to such a significant degree by customers. We become accustomed to the new higher standard.

For example, I landed at Chicago's O'Hare with no ride planned. That would not have been the case a relatively short time ago. Not wanting to deal with long cab lines—particularly in bad weather—whenever I had business in Chicago, I always made a reservation for a ride to downtown well before my arrival. This time, while walking through the airport and dragging my carry-on, I whipped out my iPhone and connected with Uber. I instantly ordered my ride. What was amazing in the not too distant past is now standard operating procedure.

What does this mean for a disruptor?

For disruptors to become iconic companies, they will have to find a way to continue to advance and enhance both their promises and their performance—or they will fall into another category.

After a long road trip, the last thing I want to do when I finally return home is to go out to a restaurant. However, there's no way that my wife wants to cook another meal for herself after being home alone for several days. What do we do? Well, sometimes—if we're both feeling brave—I do the cooking. However, more often than not, I don't want to cook because I'm tired from my travel. In those cases, we use Uber Eats. She doesn't have to cook, and I don't have to leave the house.

The disruptor Uber raised the bar with its instant car service and then expanded their promise from "taking you where you want to go" into "*and* we can bring your favorite food to your door, so you don't have to go anywhere." By enhancing and expanding their promise—and performing at a high level by executing on those promises—they continue to disrupt.

Uber has also recently announced Uber Health. Uber recognizes that transportation is one of the challenges for some patients in receiving proper care. Caregivers, patients, and staff may find easier access to their doctors and clinics by utilizing the Uber system of drivers and technology. They've even made it possible to access Uber Health without a smartphone to be of greater service to senior citizens, who may not possess the latest in technology. It's another way that Uber continues to expand both the promise and performance of the company.[33]

I realize that it's possible that you—and probably others that you know—have had an inferior personal experience with Uber, Amazon, or any of the companies that I'm writing about. The important point is that while no organization is perfect, Uber usually works as it promises and Amazon usually delivers to your door on time. Performance—like beauty—is in the eye of the beholder.

Most of us behold that they're doing it right, but I recognize that "your mileage may vary" in your personal experience.

What happens when you can't keep up?

When *Sports Illustrated* was founded, a weekly magazine devoted exclusively to sports was highly disruptive in the publishing marketplace. The problem was that *SI* believed their promise was to "publish a magazine on sports." What the customer wanted was "sports information." Enter ESPN. The cable sports network filled the gap and raised the bar. *Sports Illustrated* was woefully unprepared to expand and enhance their promise. Despite forays into television with CNN and other very modest efforts at innovation, they were late to the game. Sadly, *SI* is swiftly falling into irrelevancy. Concurrently, other new entries like Barstool Sports are growing a raving fan base—ironically consisting of the very engaged sports enthusiasts who would make up the natural market that *Sports Illustrated* previously attracted.

In the case of *SI*, the disruptor eventually became a laggard. *How do you keep this from happening to you?*

It's not enough to evaluate if your promise is relevant in today's marketplace. Rather, evaluate whether your promise is compelling in today's marketplace.

In chapter 8, we'll look at the steps that organizations and leaders can take to regain iconic status if they discover their position has slipped in the market.

Manipulators (Low Promise, High Performance)

You read that correctly. If you consistently underpromise and overdeliver, you aren't *serving* today's customer—you're attempting to *manipulate* them.

Don't misunderstand me—I am *not* suggesting that you stop making strides to create Ultimate Customer Experiences by doing the extra steps that create high levels of customer engagement.

If you're a service department at an auto dealership, this does not mean you stop vacuuming the floorboards or putting a rose on the seat. If you're a B2B company, it doesn't mean that you halt the practice of taking your best client to a sporting event or nice dinner. Whatever you're doing to ensure an experience that thrills and amazes your customers or clients, *keep it up!*

The point here is that I've learned that many organizations skew their promises so the company is set up to exceed their performance for the customer.

Many organizations skew their promises so the company is set up to exceed their performance for the customer.

It's an insincere attempt to become a hero.

Let's say Ms. Smith takes her car to the auto dealership for an oil change. She's told that her car will be ready at 5:00 p.m. Later that afternoon, the service advisor calls his customer. "Ms. Smith, great news! It's only 3:00 p.m. and your car is ready. Because you're such a valued customer, we wanted to exceed your expectations here at Jones Auto!"

The problem is that Ms. Smith has made plans to pick up her kids at the sitter at six, because she was told her car would be ready at five. The extra two-hour window means nothing to her in terms of convenience. If she would have known that her car could have been completed by three, she would have made arrangements at work and skipped paying for a couple of extra hours for her kids to be with the sitter. This "overdeliver" from the dealership has cost her both time and money.

Ms. Smith also notices that the dealership seems to do this every time she takes her car in for service. It seems that getting the car done ahead of time is just a gimmick that she's getting tired of. In other words, the precise activity that the dealership presumes is positive is, in fact, reducing the level of trust that the customer has in them.

Hmm, she might be thinking. *If they're that phony when it comes to service, could they also be playing games with me when I buy my car there?*

A hotel chain where I often stay never has an upgrade available when I make a reservation online. They can almost never let me check in early and cannot promise they will ever allow me to check out late . . . until I arrive onsite. Once I get there, they always are able to do all the above. Don't get me wrong—I appreciate being able to get into my room early and have access to the room a little bit after posted checkout time to change after a speech into something more casual for the trip home. It's just that I know they can easily let me check in a little early and check out a little late. It's not really "overde-livery," but they want me to *feel* like it is. They're trying to manipulate me.

"Oh, no, sir. We could not possibly accept reserva-tions at this late juncture for a table on a Saturday night!" you are told. "We are a very popular restaurant. You are free, however, to stop by and see if there is a cancellation or if we could squeeze you in."

The first couple of times you show up and attempt to dine there, the restaurant discovers to great astonishment that they can "squeeze you in." Naturally, you have a pos-itive feeling about the establishment. However, when they to do it every time and you repeatedly notice empty tables after being informed they have no availability, you realize it's just a ploy.

I'll say it again: it's important to deliver the Ultimate Customer Experience, but don't repeatedly underpromise and overdeliver. Your efforts become undervalued by the customers you want to impress and in doing so you take your focus off what really matters: *doing what you said you would do when you said you would do it.*

In a study conducted by behavior scientists at University of California San Diego, they found that

- keeping a promise increases its *perceived value*;
- exceeding a promise is less important than keeping one; and
- keeping a promise has a more positive outcome than exceeding one.[34]

When your performance is congruent with your promise, it delivers the outcomes you desire. When you exceed the promise with your performance, your efforts are undervalued by the customers you seek to impress.

The study found that people place a high value on people (or companies) who keep their promises—and that there is no added value for exceeding the promise.

It might be hard to keep your promise, but it's definitely worth it.

The results go on to show that "it is wise to invest effort in keeping a promise because breaking it can be costly, but it may be unwise to invest additional effort to exceed one's promises. When companies, friends, or coworkers put forth the effort to keep a promise, their effort is likely to be rewarded. But when they expend extra effort in order to exceed those promises, their effort appears likely to be overlooked."[35]

If we are overdelivering when it comes to enhancing the service experience, customers tend to appreciate it as long as it does not become the standard operating procedure. If it does, customers recognize the game and share their experiences with one another on social media.

The fundamental question is: are you promising and performing or manipulating?

PROS AND CONS OF EACH GROUP

Obviously, each group can have positives—and, they all have negatives as well.

Group	Pros	Cons
Laggards	deliver what they promise	fail to promise or deliver anything significant

Group	Pros	Cons
Frauds	excite us with the promise	deceive us regarding ability to deliver
Disruptors	change the game with promises	must continue to advance the promise and performance
Manipulators	engage us with higher performance than promised	eventually creates distrust because of consistent discrepancies

If each of these groups have their faults, where do iconic companies fall on the scale? What do they do to maintain their status?

Most iconic companies would fall in a sweet spot somewhere in the bottom left quarter of the disruptor quadrant. Their promises are slightly more aggressive and advanced from the pack. And they perform at a higher level than others, not only in their specific industry but in the entire marketplace.

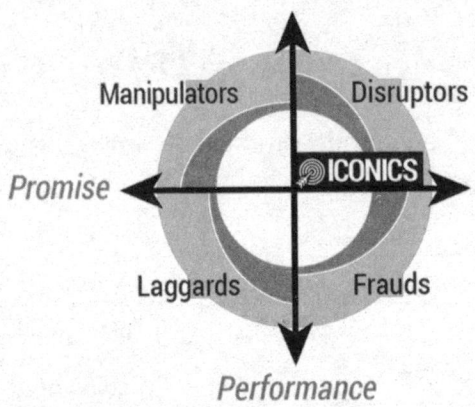

THE SWEET SPOT

As with any matrix, there are variations within any specific group. For example, some manipulators may wildly overdeliver and underpromise more than others. Nonetheless, both would fit into the category.

Iconic companies typically are going to be found in the disruptor quadrant. However, in most cases, they are going to be neither radically promising nor outrageously delivering. They constantly are looking to improve and expand upon their promises.

An example would be Uber's efforts to add restaurant delivery and helping you make it to health care appointments. And they don't skimp on performance either, like Amazon making sure my friend received his package on race day in Indiana. This runs true with the Scottsdale Princess too. After establishing their resort as *the* place for Christmas, they are now striving to become the go-to destination for other holidays.

Iconic companies find a way to
accelerate their promises while
improving their performance to
a public that has already become
predisposed to expect their excellence.

WHAT DO *YOU* DO NEXT?

Briefly, here are the five steps you need to be taking to move your organization—and yourself—closer towards iconic status:

1. Examine your promises
2. Evaluate your performance
3. Create strategies and tactics for alignment
4. Advance your promises
5. Accelerate your performance

1) EXAMINE YOUR PROMISES

Take a close look at what you are promising your customers and employees. As we discussed earlier in this chapter, examine what is the most prevalent customer perception regarding those promises. Is the promise you are making compelling to customers and/or employees? Is the promise one that you will be able to fulfill?

You should be coordinating throughout the organization—or your department or team—to ensure that everyone is on board and committed to your promise.

2) EVALUATE YOUR PERFORMANCE

Assess your performance based on your customers' perception of your promise. Is it possible that customers think you are good at your performance—just not in a manner that is congruent with your promise?

A fast food franchise may measure success based on the speed at which the customer proceeds through the drive-thru line and reward the performance accordingly. Customers, however, believe the promise includes receiving the right order in the bag. If Apple evaluates itself based on the technological quality of its devices, they will naturally believe that they are delivering extraordinarily well for me. The problem is, as I mentioned earlier, I thought the promise was "ease of use."

The old saw is that "you can only manage what you can measure." The challenge is that you need to be measuring the right elements to create customer loyalty and engagement.

Don't just evaluate how your team is performing; evaluate how they are performing based on the customer's perception of your promise.

3) CREATE STRATEGIES AND TACTICS THAT ALIGN

In a previous book, I wrote about organizations that have had a less-than-successful quarter or year and decide the problem is that they aren't as productive as they should be. With that in mind, they double down: salespeople are required to make more contacts with clients, call centers must handle more in-bound conversations, and marketing is pressured to come up with more creative advertisements.

For many, the problem is that they are
working harder on the wrong plan.

Instead of pushing more intensely to achieve what has already left your customers and prospects indifferent, why not use this as the time to ensure your strategies and tactics are in alignment?

Every customer can probably tell you a story about seeing an advertisement about "great customer service" but are placed on "hold" for twenty minutes every time they call for assistance. Don't permit your team or company to be perceived as a fraud! Make sure your performance matches your promises before you do anything else.

4) ADVANCE YOUR PROMISES

Now that you've taken the first three steps, you can examine how to advance your promises. Just as Uber did with health care and food delivery, just as the Fairmont Scottsdale Princess is doing with other holidays, you can do with your team or organization.

It's not about being revolutionary or chaotic at this juncture. It's about taking a step to set yourself apart.

For example: in my company, my team schedules a conference call with every new client. This helps me learn more about their organization and ascertain their goals for my presentation so I can customize my talk to their specific event. As you might imagine, this is standard procedure for every speaker. We decided to see how we could advance our promises. We started promising that my programs would be not only highly customized—we would also offer something to every audience member before and after each event.

Our clients loved this. It meant their investment in a keynote speaker would have greater impact than just the hour I was typically on stage. They knew I wasn't just delivering a "canned" speech and the impact of the meeting would extend beyond just the conference.

Advancing our promise gained attention in the marketplace, served as a terrific sales tool, and demonstrated our understanding of the challenges our clients were facing.

5) Accelerate your performance

It's not enough to advance your promises. You must accelerate your performance to match. Remember, you must do what you said you will do.

This can be done by departments, teams, leaders, and organizations—no matter their size or industry.

So what did we do to deliver on our advanced promise? We now provide our clients with a survey for everyone to complete before the event. This short (usually four-question) survey not only helps me learn what my audience is concerned about before the speech, it also gives me the ability to say to them at the beginning of my talk, "Here's what *you* indicated were important issues, and I constructed this program to what *you* identified as critical." Following each presentation, I shoot a short video recapping my talk. Our client then sends that video to each audience member.

The results have been fantastic: more repeat and referral business, deeper engagement with clients, the privilege of being of greater assistance to our customers, and more profitability for our company.

It's not remaking the business; it's simply finding and delivering advanced promises and accelerated performance for your customers in ways that make a difference for them. You can do the same!

WHAT'S NEXT?

Getting your promise and performance aligned is critical—and one step where you need to spend resources that are more important than money. Your investment of *time* and *commitment* is essential. However, if you execute on this step, you may create iconic results!

Now that I have my promise and performance congruent, you might be thinking, *I'm ready to start pushing my products and services, right?*

Wrong. And that leads us to the next step.

Questions for Chapter 4

- What is the promise that you are making to your customers? Is this what they perceive it to be?
- How do you believe that your customers view your performance? Is it congruent with your promise?
- What group do you believe you fit into? In which group would you choose to be placed?

  o   Laggard?
  o   Fraud?
  o   Disruptor?
  o   Manipulator?

- How can you accelerate your promise?
- What does it take to advance your performance?
- What can we do starting today to move closer to iconic status?

CHAPTER FIVE

#3 STOP SELLING

Let me start by freely admitting that of course you cannot cease selling and survive, much less become an iconic organization or leader.

The problem is that too many people emphasize the old-school, hard-sell approach to selling. They fail to recognize that times have changed dramatically. Arm-twisting, "always be closing," and "getting the prospect to surrender" tactics will cost you and your company more sales than you gain through your aggression.

Stop it.

SELLING IS NOT ABOUT SELLING

My friend, Ian Altman, has a great idea: sell like an expert, not like a salesperson. "Effective sales," according to Altman, "is not about persuasion or coercion, it's about getting to the truth as quickly as possible."[36]

Notice how his philosophy tracks so well with the "attraction" aspect we discussed in chapter 1? We are

117

attracted to take the advice of experts; we are repelled at being pushed into a purchase.

Leigh Ashton is a top sales consultant and speaker who works for Sasudi, a sales training organization. She wrote, "Selling is *not about selling*. It means simply the art of selling has moved on from the 'always be closing,' 'sell anything to anyone and to hell with the consequences' era."[37]

> *Iconic organizations and professionals have grown beyond the need to hawk their products and services.*

Iconic organizations and professionals have grown beyond the need to hawk their products and services. In fact, many would be embarrassed if customers perceived that was their customary practice. Again, this does *not* mean that they don't make an effort to sell their products or services. It's that they realize making the sale isn't the end game. Building a relationship is.

Porsches, for example, are purchased through dealerships and from the sales professionals who work there. Successfully concluding transactions and turning prospects into customers in no way diminishes Porsche's iconic status. In fact, they'd be bankrupt without it. However, the Porsche salesperson is taught to be committed to providing the best service he or she can because the reputation of the almost ninety-year-old automaker depends upon it.

When executed properly, I truly believe that there is no professional more admirable and beneficial to a customer than a salesperson. If the salesperson is assisting the customer correctly and the product or service delivers as promised, then he or she is improving the customer's life in some manner and stands a good chance of establishing a long-term relationship.

To stop selling is to understand growth
comes from building the relationship
and enhancing the experience—not
overwhelming the customer with aggressive
prospecting or closing techniques.

The Importance of the Experience

More times than I care to remember, I've had sales professionals or managers challenge me on this. They suggest the old saw that service is the first step of the next sale—as if the *experience* did not contribute to making the initial sale possible. That's asinine!

While you may have seen these (or similar) statistics quoted previously, now is a good time to review the importance of the customer experience in generating sales for your organization:

- According to the [customer experience research firm] Temkin Group, 86 percent of those who received an excellent customer experience were likely to repurchase from that company, compared to only 13 percent of those who had a very poor customer experience (*more than 6 times more likely*).
- The Temkin Group also found that those who received excellent customer experiences were *11 times more likely to recommend the company* than those who had a very poor customer experience (77 percent vs. 7 percent, respectively).
- Forrester Research found that customer experience leaders grow revenue faster than laggards, with leaders seeing a *17 percent compound average revenue growth rate*, compared to only 3 percent for their customer experience laggard counterparts.
- When it comes to down competing on price or the experience, Gartner found that 64 percent of people found customer experience to be *more important than price* when it comes to purchasing something.[38]

> The critical aspect is that iconic businesses
> know that enhancing the experience
> increases sales.

Can you imagine Apple having a "get out there and crush it" sales campaign? Imagine a semicrazed, half-balding salesman in front of boxes upon boxes of Macintosh computers, shouting, "We've stacked them deep and we're selling them cheap!"? Not in this lifetime, I'll wager.

Yet many companies would rather take that approach than do what it takes to create iconic status for their organization. Their leaders prefer hammering their sales force to push harder to sell than to encourage their teams to build a greater experience. Don't think that's the case? Then ask yourself these two questions:

1. When was our last sales rally or meeting?
2. When was our last customer experience meeting?

I know a plethora of companies with annual sales meetings that have *never* had a customer experience conference. Then they wonder why neither sales nor customer loyalty are growing. "Customers' expectations have fundamentally changed," said Lynn Vojvodich, board member for Ford Motor Company and Priceline Group and former CMO of Salesforce.com. "They want you to know who they are, what they've bought, and what they like. So, if you cold call them and don't have any information about their company and their industry—if you don't know what they've purchased, what they called for service help on—they're going to hang up on you."[39]

Why, then, don't all companies focus on the experience?

> *It's easier to berate sales teams to work harder and to cut your prices than it is to stop selling and build iconic experiences through customer relationships.*

Many organizations—and their leaders—typically prefer to take what they see as the path of least resistance. This is especially true in smaller businesses where an entrepreneurial founder may have vast experience in his respective industry—but little training in creating the Ultimate Customer Experience.

THE "EASY" PATH IS COSTLY

This ridiculous practice is seen every day on social media—and, perhaps, especially on LinkedIn. Consider this example from a spam message I recently received—along with my comments.

Message	Comments
Hi Scott,	1) I find a comma in the salutation on the initial message you send me to be a bit informal and perhaps unprofessional. Not a good start.
This is Anne of XYX Central. I was wondering if you're available for a chat.	2) You've told me nothing about why I would be interested. Why would you ask me to invest my time as the very first point in your message?
I'm reaching out to see if your company would be interested in finding new clients.	3) Ugh! What a trite, manipulative line. "I'm wondering if you'd like to improve your profitability?" is another. Do you really believe your prospect is *that* stupid? If you do, you're too dumb to be selling to them.
Our services can reach out to your target audience not only by calling but also email and LinkedIn messaging.	4) So you're offering to spam my prospects the way you are spamming me? Anne, you have given me zero indication that you have any idea what I do. So how do you know anything about my "target audience" or what I need to do to "reach out" to them? And nothing you have told me assures me you have the experience and depth to be able to do so.
Allow us to do the complex and tedious legwork of sales and marketing for you so you can focus on what you do best—improving your products and services and closing deals.	5) Anne, you have no idea what my products and services are. How can you possibly know that improving them or closing the sale is what I do best?)

Message	Comments
It will only take a brief phone call with us to discuss the details of this opportunity. Is your calendar open on Tuesday at 1:30 PM for a quick call? Please let me know what's the best number to reach you.	6) Why should I block my calendar to educate you? This is your opportunity for you to sell me—it's not an "opportunity" for me at this point. I know nothing about you

This is beyond cold calling— it's more like frigid pleading.

Observe the aspects of her message that are so off-putting to a prospect. For example, in point 6 above, notice how she wants to set up a call with me to pick my brain and prequalify my prospective clients. She should have done that homework before spamming me! In other words, it appears she knows just one aspect about me: I have an account on LinkedIn. There's nothing in her message that indicates she knows anything about my potential problems or needs. She wants me to commit to investing my time to help her do what she should have done before initial contact. This is incredibly distasteful to a prospect. Don't ever do it.

Remember the earlier line quoted from Lynn Vojvodich? "If you cold call them and don't have any information about their company and their industry, they're going to hang up on you."[40]

Which is what I did to Anne. I asked to be removed from her mailing list. However, it's worse for Anne's company than that. I've *blocked* her. I don't have time for spam. It means that because of this effort on her part to "sell" me, she doesn't get a second opportunity to try to serve me.

While we have never met personally, I am connected through social media and mutual friends to a *New York Times* bestselling author who also owns a company that helps aspiring authors get published. He was contacted on LinkedIn by a publishing company that asked him, "Have you ever considered publishing a book?"

The author posted the ridiculous message and called out the spammer online. He received a plethora of venomous responses telling him, in essence, "Sales is a numbers game" or "If you don't like it, too bad. This is the future." My take is that if you send a stupid spam message to someone, you should be prepared for any consequences. And the consequence of the easy path can be a lost relationship—or even worse, a bad reputation.

THE PROBLEM WITH THE NUMBERS GAME

Is there is a relationship between number of outbound calls or emails and sales?

When you're sending out thousands of messages, you get the metric on how many opens, clicks, and responses that your missives have received. You may naturally assume that if you send out thousands more, you'll hit on more companies or people who need what you're selling.

Unfortunately, you're only seeing one side of the equation.

Imagine for a moment that you have created the first antiviral drug that cures the flu. You inject people who have come down with the flu. To your amazement and gratification, for every one thousand people to whom you give the shot, four hundred are completely cured of the flu. You're really on to something, aren't you?

Perhaps. However, first you need to know if the drug is causing any unintended side effects. What if four hundred are cured from the flu, but the medication is simultaneously killing five hundred from heart attacks? Would you still administer it?

Professional spammers know the metrics on clicks and responses. What they often *don't* know is how many prospects are so turned off that the seller will never get another chance. Do you really want that many upset prospects?

Sure, it's easy to hit send and fog your sales pitch to tens of thousands and then see who clicks. Unfortunately, it is just as easy to ignore the collateral damage you're causing because it's usually less obvious and often not immediately painful.

In situations like this, prospects go so far as to become a "reverse referral." These are people who go out of their way—in person and on social media—to strongly recommend that people *not* do business with you. How many sales will the path of least resistance cost you over the long haul?

The first time I posted my disapproval of these types of inane messages on LinkedIn, I received a response berating me for my attitude. "If you're so smart," the responder's message implied, "how would you do it?" Well, the message just so happened to be from a sales professional in a city where I had lived years ago. He worked at a car dealership where I had purchased multiple automobiles when I lived there. It turns out I also knew a relative of his. The salesman had no idea he just alienated a person who had spent tens of thousands of dollars with his employer—and he was probably going to hear about it from his family too! (You can almost hear the song, "It's a Small World After All" playing in the background, can't you?)

All it would have taken was just a couple of moments to enter my name into the dealership database just to be certain he wasn't about to offend a customer. It seems as though when it comes to hitting the send button on posts and tweets, we have a new mantra: "Fire . . . Ready . . . Aim." Some want to immediately put in their two cents to get their point across—and perhaps even troll the person whose views are in opposition—without considering the bigger picture of how this makes one appear.

It's not just those idiots with "keyboard courage" who cowardly hide behind anonymous avatars and rip everything to shreds. It's also marketers who spam without thinking of the consequences—and then are somehow offended when someone calls them out over their errors. Others can make these mistakes—don't be that guy or gal . . . or organization.

You're aiming for iconic.

How Do You Stop Selling?

Iconic organizations take a more difficult path.

For example, I also receive a lot of sales messages from Amazon. Yet each one says something like, "Here are some recommendations based on your past purchases." Or "If you liked that . . . you'll love this!" The subtle message is, "We *know* you—that's why we are advocating these options."

As my great friends Scott and Alison Stratten—authors of several books, including *UnSelling: The New Customer Experience*—say, "Stop selling; start engaging." It cannot be expressed better than that!

When we engage, we attract. When we attract, as mentioned previously, the results are relationships with high lifetime value in terms of both repeat and referral business. Yet in my experience many people would rather rush into getting business without investing the time and effort required to build the relationship. It's like asking someone to marry you on the first date! There must be engagement and relationship-building first. Pushing hard and fast too early can propel your prospect away. It's akin to saying "Trust me" in the first moments in the initial conversation with someone. If you feel compelled to beg for their trust so quickly, you've raised the issue that maybe there's a reason that they shouldn't.

So how do you slow down and build a relationship instead? Here are three steps to stop selling and approach prospects the way iconic leaders and companies do:

1. Appeal to their aspirations—then invite them to savor the experience
2. Provide value before an ask
3. Stop thinking like a professional

APPEAL TO THEIR ASPIRATIONS—THEN INVITE THEM TO SAVOR THE EXPERIENCE

The Fairmont Scottsdale Princess almost never discusses specific room rates in their marketing materials. Instead, they appeal to what you would like to do for a fun break at a wonderful resort—or a productive meeting at a prominent conference center—and then invite you to partake in that experience. They present pictures of their Trailblazer's Kids Club and show young people—maybe children just like yours—having a great time. They share shots of gorgeous weddings held on the property—maybe just like the one you and your fiancé desire.

How does that differ from a sales pitch?

First, unlike the spam email, it requires zero commitment from me.

Second, in almost a subliminal manner, it appeals to something I may desire and *attracts* me, rather than tries to push me into staying there. Their visuals assure me they will successfully accomplish my goals for my stay, that if I go there with my meeting or my family, I'm going to savor a superior experience.

How can you appeal to your prospects' wants, needs, desires, and aspirations—and invite them to partake in your experience?

Consider the Volkswagen Group Australia and the amazing way it drives (pardon the pun) this type of customer experience—in an industry primarily known for anything but. The Volkswagen dealers in Australia promise to provide "Premium for the People." Who doesn't want a premium level of automobile service, and dealership experience? And "for the people" suggests that it's accessible to everyone, so VW invites you to join them and experience what they have to offer.

If you run a transmission repair shop, don't talk about fixing the car. Appeal to the aspiration of safe transportation and a car that doesn't break down on the side of the road in a bad part of town. If you own a dry cleaner, don't get caught up in a race to the bottom on the price of laundering a shirt. Appeal to the aspiration of looking great at work, school, or a party. In every case, clearly demonstrate how you will provide a superior experience that the customer will want to encounter for herself.

Appeal to the aspirations of your customers and prospects. Then invite them to savor the experience that they desire through your product or service.

PROVIDE VALUE *BEFORE* AN ASK

Legendary motivational speaker and broadcaster Earl Nightingale, known as the dean of personal development, used to say many people sell like someone sitting before a woodstove. "If you give me some heat," they say, "then I'll put in some wood."

That's the case with many marketers. It's like they are saying to their cars, "If you will drive me to where I want to go, then I'll fill you up with gasoline." How many sales pitches do you receive that ask you to do something before the organization or sales professional will make a commitment?

"Is your calendar open on Tuesday at 1:30 p.m. for a quick call? Please let me know what's the best number to reach you." That's what was requested in the LinkedIn sales pitch from someone I've never been contacted by before. Why should I invest my time in something that may have zero return?

The prospect who talks to you has made an investment whether she buys or not. She has invested something more precious and valuable than money—her time and attention. Yet that investment seems so lightly valued by so many who just keep on selling (or attempting to sell, anyway.)

> *Iconic companies get the order right. They provide value first and then ask for your time.*

While author, speaker, and internet personality Gary Vaynerchuk may be perceived as the aggressive, pushy type when you watch his style on social media, there's no doubt he has it exactly right when it comes to the "value first, ask next" philosophy.

"My entire business philosophy pretty much revolves around the 'jab jab jab right hook' method," Vaynerchuk writes. "Jabs are the value you provide your customers with: the content you put out, the good things you do to convey your appreciation. And the right hook is the ask: it's when you go in for the sale, ask for a subscribe, ask for a donation. You've got to throw several jabs before you throw your hook. [And], just because you jab and jab and jab doesn't mean you automatically get to land the right hook. It just allows you to have the audacity to ask. You have to earn the right to ask people for a sale. In fact, you have to earn the right to ask people for anything. That's just life."[41]

Vaynerchuk cites iconic contemporary performer Taylor Swift as an example of someone who provided value to fans first. Among the many things Swift has done for fans, she

- got tickets for a fan who missed her flight tickets to another sold-out show,
- made a playlist for a fan who was sad over a breakup,
- donated to a family's Kickstarter campaign after a horrific car accident, and
- tracked down a fan who waited in the cold for 20 hours for tickets and took a selfie with her.[42]

Scott Swift, Taylor's father, was in the audience for one of my speeches years ago prior to his daughter's becoming a pop icon. He related to me many instances where Taylor had reached out to her then small group of fans before she achieved global recognition. I've thought of our conversation often in the years that have followed. Even as a teenager, Taylor Swift intuitively knew that if you want more fans, start by treating the ones you already have amazingly well. By offering all those jabs, as Gary Vaynerchuk calls them, because she first provided such terrific value and experiences for her fans, guess what they did when she later gave them a right hook, or asked them to buy her next release of new music?

What is the specific value that should you provide? Obviously that depends on your product or service. This method works, however, regardless of what business you are in.

The Ultimate Business Summit is a program for entrepreneurs that two of my friends—bestselling authors and Hall of Fame professional speakers Larry Winget and Randy Pennington—and I host annually in Las Vegas. We help small businesses create this values-based, results-oriented, distinctive approach. We have landscapers in our seminars who are now doing videos on YouTube on how you should plant your spring flowers, chimney sweeps posting blogs about fire dangers in your home, and specialty food companies doing podcasts on simple changes in diet that can help you feel better. In every case, both sales and profitability are growing for these small businesses because of the value they are providing to prospective customers before they ask them for anything.

You do not have to be an international behemoth like Amazon—or a company with a gorgeous setting like the Fairmont Scottsdale Princess—to make this work. All you have to do is plan, create, and deliver something of value before you invite prospects to do business with you.

STOP THINKING LIKE A PROFESSIONAL

Every business wants to sell and grow more than the competition; few actually do. Every sales professional desires to become highly successful; only a fraction really do.

What's the problem? What is stopping us from coming up with the innovative approaches required to sell more and grow our market share over the competition?

Interestingly, in 2012 some neuroscientists at the National Institute on Deafness and Other Communication Disorders in Bethesda, Maryland, conducted a study to "identify the neural correlates of spontaneous lyrical improvisation."

Twelve rappers "freestyled"—strung together unrehearsed lyrics, a difficult and highly valued skill in the world of rap music—while connected to an MRI machine. Next, Doctors Siyuan Liu and Allen Braun and their colleagues had the rappers recite memorized lyrics. Finally, the researchers compared the two sets of brain scans.

"We think what we see is a relaxation of 'executive functions' to allow more natural defocused attention and uncensored processes to occur that might be the hallmark of creativity," said Dr. Braun.

The results of the study were in line with the discoveries from previous research that Dr. Braun conducted with Charles Limb, a doctor and musician at Johns Hopkins University that looked at MRIs of jazz musicians.

This isn't about being a rapper or jazz artist. It's about how all of us think innovatively—which, of course, can have significant impact on your approach to business.

Michael Eagle, a study coauthor who raps under the name Open Mike Eagle, agrees: "That's kind of the nature of . . . improvisation. Even as people who do it, we're not 100% sure of where we're getting improvisation from."[43]

In other words, rappers and jazz musicians cannot simultaneously freestyle and analyze their performance. Without "breathing space" between innovation and evaluation, we shut down the flow of our creativity.

The article states that the study suggests there are two phases to creativity:

- Phase One is spontaneous and based upon improvisation to create unique ideas and approaches.
- Phase Two is where we process, revise, and improve our original thoughts.

What does this mean regarding your sales methods and connecting with customers?

The study illuminates the problem that when we want to become more innovative, typically our "executive function" or "sales professional" thinking quickly kicks in. In other words, we attempt to be creative and evaluate at the same time.

This frequently results in the "we've never done it that way before" or "do you know how much it would take to do that?" syndrome. We don't stretch ourselves to become spontaneous and "off the cuff." Unfortunately, we usually attempt to innovate as we simultaneously appraise and process. This kills the very type of innovation that is required to stand out in today's marketplace. Don't shut down your opportunity to be innovative in your approach by overanalyzing new methods.

Perhaps this explains why many companies typically fall back into the old methods of hardcore selling. That style may have worked thirty years ago when customers didn't have as many alternatives to that aggressive approach as they do today. However, there's little doubt that old, hardcore techniques fall woefully short of establishing the relationships that customers crave today.

Strange as it may sound, if you want to follow the lead of iconic companies and stop selling, maybe you need to think less like a business professional and, if only for a little while, think more like a rapper—let it flow.

Michelle Stacy, former president of Keurig—the famed maker of K-cups and coffee brewers—and a coaching client of mine, used this innovative strategy to make a profound impact on the company she led. If you're a coffee company and you want customers to drink your product, who would you consider as your primary competition? There's no doubt—the iconic Starbucks.

The typical, traditional "executive thinking" would ask

- How can we sell more and grow our market share in an industry dominated by such an iconic presence?
- What do we need to do to gain a foothold against Starbucks?

Stacy stopped thinking like an executive and instead decided to think first like an innovator. "What if," she asked herself, "we were *collaborators* instead of competitors?"

Consider how revolutionary that approach would be considered in her industry. It's the CEO of Ford asking how they could do more business with GM. It's the CEO of McDonald's asking how they could partner with KFC. It's Steve Jobs asking how he could collaborate with Bill Gates. (Oh, wait! That one really *happened*. Just another example of "rapper think.")

Michelle Stacy decided that instead of fighting the traditional industry battles, she could innovate. She would get Starbucks into Keurig's K-cups. The results were astounding. K-cups and brewer sales grew, making Keurig happy. Starbucks had an additional revenue stream, making them thrilled. The innovative collaboration increased sales for both companies.

In other words, Michelle Stacy sold more when she stopped selling.

IT'S NOT ALL A HAPPY PLACE

It's not easy to stop selling and start focusing on the experience. As my friend Jason Bradshaw, chief customer officer and director at Volkswagen Group Australia, says, "It takes a lot of energy and focus to move from a very product-centered industry to one that matches its product experience with a seller/customer experience as well."

While most would look for a positive approach to this challenge, the next chapter may provide you with a controversial alternative. In fact, I'm positive that you should go negative.

Questions for Chapter 5

- How do you sell your products and services? Would you describe your efforts as primarily pushing—or engaging?
- On a scale of 1 to 10 (10 being the best), how would you rate your customer retention? How could you enhance the experience of doing business with you to the iconic level so you could retain more customers?
- On a scale of 1 to 10 (10 being the best), how would you rate the amount of referral business you are receiving from current customers? How could you enhance the experience and inspire more customers to refer you to their friends and colleagues?
- How do you appeal to the aspirations of your customers and prospects? What could you do to improve?
- What are you currently doing to provide information, insight, and value to the marketplace—even to prospects who are not yet customers? How could you provide more value to your customers—*before asking for a sale?*
- Develop three innovative ideas about your business. They do not have to be practical or something you could start doing today. Explain how these ideas would attract more customers to you (or better employees to work with you).

CHAPTER SIX

#4 GO NEGATIVE

Now is the time in many business books where—after you've navel gazed at your "why" and read all of the wonderous stories about how Disney, Starbucks, Amazon, and Apple make their customers and employees so "happy"—the author suggests that this positive approach is the key to your future success.

Surprisingly, that's not what iconic companies do. Instead, they go negative.

Leaders who are constantly putting on a happy face and organizations always seeking a sunny outlook may be taking the wrong approach. Consider these shocking facts:

- "A study of data from British households found that across two decades, especially optimistic self-employed people earned about 25 percent less than their pessimistic peers."

- "National Cancer Institute researchers found that people who lowballed their risk of heart disease were more likely to show early signs of it."
- "Married couples who were extremely optimistic about their relationship's future were more likely to experience relationship deterioration."
- "Homeowners who underestimated their chances of radon exposure were less likely to buy radon test kits than were those with a more realistic sense of risk—their optimism left them vulnerable."[44]

It seems natural to want to overlook or gloss over our own faults. We frequently work exceedingly hard at developing our strengths, making it difficult to then examine where we are falling short. In fact, managers in many organizations view merely discussing areas in need of improvement as a sign of weakness in the employee.

Ironically, not drilling deeply enough on our weaknesses is a limitation that holds back companies. In the 1960s, consultant Albert Humphrey at the Stanford Research Institute came up with the SWOT analysis. As you probably know, SWOT stands for: Strengths, Weaknesses, Opportunities, Threats. The typical approach of this method is to discuss and dissect where our team, department, or organization stands in each of the four categories.

The challenge is that frequently, we don't focus enough on our specific weaknesses.

A friend of mine who manages a sales team wanted to poll her department to determine their strengths, weaknesses, opportunities, and threats. They are in the tech industry, so they constantly face a lot of threats and disruption. Here is an example of the results of their brainstorming:

Strengths	Weaknesses
Well-recognized brand in marketplace	Brand not as innovative as competition
Young team of energetic sales professionals	Sales team lacks depth of experience
Opportunities	**Threats**
Expanding market means more sales	40% of revenue from 8% of clients
Many clients with old equipment to replace	Competition investing more in R&D

We know that most professionals are reluctant to admit shortcomings. However, it is even harder during a SWOT analysis because we are called upon to identify our weaknesses and threats immediately after the excitement of noting our most important strengths.

My friend learned to be careful when using a SWOT. The problem she discovered is that underestimating weaknesses can be more dangerous than overestimating assets.

An article by John Humphreys, associate professor of management in the College of Business and Technology at Texas A&M University in the *MIT Sloan Management Review,* agrees:

> "In fact, the notion of discussing weaknesses has become anathema to strategy formulation in many companies. Too many senior executives simply do not want to talk about them. Doing so is often seen as admitting defeat and appearing vulnerable. Organizational leaders must bear some of the responsibility for ignoring weakness. But many who consult in this area also share some of the blame by referring to everything the company lacks as an opportunity. We know managers recoil at the term weakness, so opportunity becomes a generic pit into which a broad continuum of true opportunities and veiled weaknesses are tossed. I've even witnessed a SWOT-analysis session where poor brand image was earnestly listed as an opportunity. Nonsense! Although the possibility for improvement may (or may not) exist, poor brand image clearly puts the company at a disadvantage when compared to competitors. Moreover, falsely labeling true weaknesses as opportunities actually puts the company at greater risk."[45]

This is not to suggest that iconic leaders or companies have what we would commonly call a "negative attitude." They *don't*. Instead, this should emphasize that iconic companies and leaders are not *afraid* of the negative. Rather, they *welcome* it as part of the process of creating, sustaining, or regaining iconic status. They are as intent on discovering customer dissatisfaction as finding out what pleases and satisfies those who do business with them.

WHAT INFURIATES YOUR CUSTOMERS?

Before we proceed, a bit of a confession. It took me a while to write this section because when I speak and write, I've always tried to use nonoffensive language. As the late great Zig Ziglar once told me, "No one will ever come up and say how much they loved all those times you cursed during your presentations. But people will come up after every one of them to tell you how much they appreciated that you kept it clean." I have always taken Zig's advice to heart.

While many have no problem with coarse language—and, I'll admit that I've been known to swear occasionally in personal conversation—others instinctively recoil at it.

When customers get bad service, are treated rudely, or are insulted, there really is only one way to describe their response: they are pissed off.

When you have terrible customer service, you probably don't find yourself saying, "The way you've treated me as a customer is an *affront*" or "I find myself *in a tizzy* over this situation with your company!"

My wife, Tammy, suggested I say, "ticked off," "grinds their gears," or "chaps their cheeks." While I appreciate her suggestions, I have to maintain that none of those phrases quite capture the intensity that a highly offended customer feels. I'm sorry if I offend you with that comment, but this isn't about mere irritation. It's more than friction that the customer experiences in the process of doing business. There's something about that term that connects with our deep-seated outrage and infuriation about having to deal with a problem that usually has no reason for existing.

I guess I'm saying that I hope I won't "chap your cheeks" because I'm using the term "pissed off."

However, I am also strongly advocating that if you don't know what is pissing off your customers—or your employees—you will never achieve iconic status.

Ask yourself what pisses you off when *you're* the customer.

Last night Tammy was at a dinner function, so I went to a local Mexican restaurant to dine alone. The place was packed, so I sat in the bar area. When a server finally approached me, she asked abruptly, "Know what you're having tonight?" I smiled and responded that a menu and water would be a great first step.

My dinner order took an exceedingly long time to arrive—and was a bit cold when it did. It obviously had been sitting in the kitchen for a while with no one to run it out to my seat. The person who placed the plate in front of me—I assumed it was the manager—vanished quickly before I had the chance to say anything. When I addressed the problem with the server, she said, "Well, it's not my fault. I turned the order in right after you told me what you wanted." When I asked to speak with the manager, she told me it would be a while; he was busy. To add insult to injury, the server made no adjustment on my bill. I was expected to pay full price for everything. There was no offer to "make it right."

While still in my seat, I went on Yelp and gave the place a scathing review.

My gears weren't just ground, my cheeks weren't just chapped—I was flat out pissed off.

Although the meal took a long time to arrive and was cold, not caring about it is the main issue. Problem in the kitchen? I may not like it, but I understand. Mistake in placing the order? It's not optimal, but it can be rectified with an apology—and maybe free dessert.

Not giving a damn? Now, you've crossed a line.

Every business has issues that are beyond their control. But, whatever the reason for poor service, *not caring about the customer* is at the heart of what *really* infuriates them.

I am sure that if a management consultant asked the team at that Mexican restaurant in a resort in the Green Valley area in Henderson, Nevada, if they cared about the customer, every employee and manager would respond with an enthusiastic, "Yes! Of course!" Their actions, however, said something different. And it was their response to the poor service that infuriated a customer who will never return and who shared his story with others. (My review had more than a thousand views on Yelp less than twelve hours later.)

> *The terrifying aspect is that there are customers and clients out there who feel the same way about your business and mine.*

Most businesses and leaders want to know who those customers are, so they can make it right and hopefully save the sale. Iconic companies are *obsessed* with learning what they did wrong, so they can change the behavior—or process—that created the unpleasant experience in the first place.

In chapter 4 we talked about how the genesis of disruption is dissatisfaction. Iconic businesses know that if they can eliminate the points of extreme dissatisfaction, they are taking steps that will erode their vulnerability to being disrupted.

How Do You Discover Points of Infuriation?

We all want to make our customers happy. The National Retail Federation released a survey indicating that among 418 executives across 137 companies in the retail industry, customer satisfaction currently is the top priority. Even if you're not in retail, there is no doubt the issue is high on your list too. Unfortunately, many leaders think it's just the behavior of employees that creates customer service issues. They tend to overlook it could be that the underlying culture of their organization isn't geared to creating iconic results. (We'll discuss that in the next chapter.)

Going negative or focusing on your company's weaknesses is not a sign of . . . well, *weakness,* but a sign of good leadership. Iconic companies view this level of introspection as a symbol of strength.

Don't be reticent to focus on the negative and ask the questions that lead to the answers we really need to move to the iconic level.

149

In 2002, a top management consulting firm, Bain & Company, developed a short consumer survey to test brand loyalty. The survey consists of one brief, simple question: "On a scale of 1 to 10, with 10 being the highest, how likely is it that you would recommend our company/product/service to a friend or colleague?" This has been called the "ultimate question" for any business to ask.[46]

Customers responding with a 9 or 10 are deemed as Promoters. They will remain loyal customers, purchase more, and tell friends and colleagues about your organization. Detractors respond with a score of 0 to 6. They aren't coming back—and they aren't referring you. They even may be actively telling colleagues and friends to stay away (like me and the Mexican restaurant.) If you answer with either a 7 or 8, you are a Passive. Your behavior is determined to fall in the middle between Promoters and Detractors.[47]

The cumulative results to this question became known as the Net Promoter Score (NPS). You learn your NPS by subtracting the percentage of customers who are designated as Detractors from the percentage of customers who are deemed to be Promoters. Passives are naturally included in the total number of respondents, which serves to lower the net score. The NPS has been advocated as "the one number you need to grow" your level of customer engagement and satisfaction—and, therefore, your business.[48]

Naturally, most organizations allow customers the opportunity to leave additional comments as they answer this short question. (This is commonly called the VOC, or "voice of the customer.") And many will follow up with those customers who respond with lower scores, so the company can "close the loop" and attempt to build a better relationship.

Some leaders and are skeptical of the simplicity of this evaluation approach. Opponents think that a single, basic question leads to overly simplistic evaluations and assumptions. They argue that NPS may not be all that accurate and that there may be a better question. Let's address these two issues.

Is NPS Accurate?

One critic of the Net Promoter Score asks: would you evaluate a student on the basis of just one test score? Or a baseball player on the basis of their batting average only? Or a car based only on its gas mileage?

These are valid and thought-provoking questions, no doubt. Yet, I have no problem with the single-question approach to customer feedback. My experience with thousands of companies over several decades is that if you make a customer survey too complex, you get no feedback. And some feedback is better than no feedback.

An obvious challenge, though, is that the NPS cannot tell you the customer's actual likelihood or influence in recommending or criticizing your business. What if meek customers are saying they'll advocate and extroverted customers are your Detractors? The end result will likely be that compelling opinion leaders will steer more people in their direction than those who gently promote your brand.

Another problem with the NPS question is that it does not tell you *why* your customers made their choice. For example: are customers saying they'll recommend you because they had a superior experience with your *product*—or because your *service* was exceptional? These are completely different aspects of your deliverables.

And what if they really aren't over the moon about a particular product or experience, but they are fans of your brand overall? That is something altogether different.

So if you aren't certain *why* they're recommending you, how do you know what specific aspects to accentuate and what needs to be improved? According to research from Stanford University, Intuit Corporation, and Harris Interactive, leaders

> need to understand whether more recommendations directly drive the growth of their business (in which case they would want to focus their efforts on directly increasing recommendations) or whether measures of likelihood of recommending are tapping into a gen-

eral attitude toward the company (which might require other efforts). In that context, it is also important to understand whether more recommendations are more important than preventing the loss of already attracted customers."[49]

There are numerous detractors that conclude that NPS is not a statistically accurate reflection of either the satisfaction of your customers or their willingness to refer you to others. Here are some key points they make:

- The standard NPS question is unipolar (willingness to recommend) but analysis treats it as bipolar (willing to detract versus willingness to promote). (Ken Roberts, Forethought Research Australia)
- NPS is attitudinal (what you say you will do) rather than behavioral (what you do) (Bird, Ehrenberg, and Barnard)
- "Satisfaction" and "liking" are better predictors of recommendations than "likelihood to recommend." ("Measuring Customer Satisfaction and Loyalty: Improving the 'Net-Promoter' Score" by Daniel Schneider, Matt Berent, Randall Thomas and Jon Krosnick)

My point here is not to be overly critical of NPS. It's to suggest that to achieve the iconic level, you must look at specific aspects of customer satisfaction and dissatisfaction to know how to improve.

With NPS, we know if they'd recommend us or not, but not what we are doing to infuriate our customers.

THERE MAY BE A BETTER QUESTION

In chapter 4, we noted the high level of customer satisfaction scores for the Apple Watch. In addition, I outlined my personal complaints—even though overall, I'm a satisfied Apple customer.

However, as I wrote in my book *What Customers REALLY Want*, when you stop to think about it, satisfaction is a pretty low standard.

Imagine being a guy about to get down on one knee, holding a box behind your back. It contains a ring that cost four months' salary. Setting things up to pop the big question, you nervously ask the person you hope will become your lifelong partner how she feels about the relationship. "Well," she responds unenthusiastically, "I guess you could mark me as satisfied"?

Is that good enough? No! You want your engagement to begin with your fiancé being amazed, thrilled, and overjoyed with the relationship!

Don't be satisfied with satisfied customers. Seek to have amazed, thrilled, and overjoyed followers.

If *satisfaction* is such a miniscule standard in personal relationships, why is it so seemingly acceptable in professional ones? Don't we want loyalty and commitment there, too?

This may be an exaggeration, but I hope it makes the point. Satisfaction isn't really *that* significant, and we don't learn much from it either.

What we really need to do is to improve our "how" by going negative and getting to the core of our weaknesses.

What if you asked every customer something like, "What have we done in the course of our relationship that has pissed you off?"

No doubt it takes courage to ask that. Having that kind of courage, though, is what sets iconic companies apart from just differentiated or even distinctive companies. Iconic companies have the confidence to learn where their errors are because they have the conviction that their team can fix them.

You want to drill deeply into the specific
points of infuriation.

Obviously you will need to customize what and how you ask your customers for honest feedback, but you should thoroughly explore where the friction is in your relationship with your customers and employees.

Apple would have received *much* more valuable information from me by asking, "What pisses you off about your Apple Watch?" than inquiring, "Would you recommend your Apple Watch to a friend?"

THE BITCH BOOK

Wanting to research this idea of customer feedback more thoroughly, I turned to social media. I asked my followers how they go about finding out what infuriates their customers about doing business with them.

One of the best ideas shared with me was from Jamie Morse, a health, wellness, and life coach who is on the volunteer leadership committee for the Relay for Life event of Queen Creek and San Tan Valley, Arizona. It's a fund-raising event for the American Cancer Society that is donation-driven and volunteer-administered.

Jaimie told me that the money raised at their event provided help to cancer patients in the community. If the event doesn't do well, they are letting down their neighbors who are battling cancer. (As someone who lost his spouse to cancer, I share her passion for this cause.)

The day of the event, Jamie placed a notebook in a central location and asked all the committee members to make notes in the book about areas where they could improve. She said if they heard anyone "bitching" about anything, they were to write it down. Thus, the notebook was dubbed the Bitch Book.

Jamie certainly wasn't afraid to go negative, but she also made it clear she wanted to know the positive, too. She asked people to also let her know if something went over really well. She finished her story with a great question: "The saying 'If it's not broke, don't fix it' is true, but how do we know if something is broken or not unless we ask?"

Customers are flocking to the Internet to voice their frustration. We've all heard of Yelp and Trip Advisor, but one website—PissedConsumer.com—reports over one million reviews of sixty-four-thousand companies from upset customers. The site claims to generate 3.5 million monthly visitors. Many customers—even those of iconic companies—are pissed off and are not reticent to share their opinions.

The question remains: *will you know who they are and have the courage to ask what caused their problem?*

POSITIVE NEGATIVITY

When I tell people they should go negative, often they have a knee-jerk response. They confuse a search for the negative *reactions* we may stimulate in others with having a negative *attitude*, which some researchers call "self-handicapping."

"Self-handicapping is a strategy with the primary aim of protecting self-esteem in the event of failure," according to researchers from the University of Rochester and Saint Mary's University.[50] We see this when leaders or organizations are so negative about potential outcomes they construct obstacles to success. This means that if—or when—failure occurs, it is attributed to the barrier rather than to any weakness of the company or management.

How many times have you heard a leader say, "There's nothing we could have done; it's the economy"? or "You just can't find good people to hire anymore"? Those are forms of self-handicapping. It's another way of saying, "It's not my fault! The economy is bad, and I have idiots working for me." Or, as we saw in the introduction, it can be executives who insist, "We didn't do anything wrong."

However, there is another form of a negative approach that researchers call "defensive pessimism." It sounds counterintuitive, but I consider it a positive approach to negativity.

For example, studies have found that in students who are apprehensive when taking important tests, it was discovered that "while pessimism is often seen as a negative trait, *defensive* pessimism can be a useful way for someone to harness their anxiety into positive results."[51]

At its core, defensive pessimism is examining what has gone—or could go—wrong, so you take the necessary steps to prevent it from occurring. This, naturally, assists in assuring a positive outcome. It is sometimes described as analyzation and overpreparation for negative outcomes to ensure positive results. Self-handicapping is expecting the worst—and being so negative that you'll prepare something to blame just in case it does.

"One thing that separates defensive pessimism from pessimism alone," researchers assert, "is that defensive pessimists . . . unlike true pessimists . . . also report a propensity to reflect about, or plan for, their performance."[52]

That's an important distinction. Defensive pessimists aren't just sitting around moping or fuming over the outcomes that have upset their customers and employees. After reflection, they are making plans to fix the problem.

Researchers identify the flip side of defensive pessimism as strategic optimism. Those employing this approach do all they can to avoid thinking about potential negative outcomes. They focus and plan for things to go right.

From observation and experience, the challenge that I often see is that those who identify themselves as strategic optimists can tend to minimize the impact that a negative experience can have upon the customer from an emotional standpoint. They find it easier to just paste on a smile and rely on the old, "We'll try harder next time" approach without directly confronting and solving the problem.

The aforementioned studies on pessimism found "Defensive pessimists show significant increases in self-esteem and satisfaction over time, perform better academically, form more supportive friendship networks, and make more progress on their personal goals than equally anxious students who do not use defensive pessimism."[53]

To be sure, defensive pessimism does not mean that we are playing defense. Rather, defensive pessimism is a method of evaluating what could go wrong—as we are on the offensive—so we can anticipate and prevent missteps.

THE MILLIONAIRE CHIMNEY SWEEP

Mark Stoner is a terrific entrepreneur. Starting as a teenager with a dream, Mark founded Ashbusters Chimney Service in Nashville, Tennessee. Mark has expanded and grown the success of his company to the point he was featured on CNBC as a "blue-collar millionaire." Yes, you read that right—a multimillionaire from his chimney sweep business.

Stoner has also founded SirVent Chimney and Venting Franchise and has served as the president of the Chimney Safety Institute of America. (He's also a member of our elite mastermind program, the Insiders Group of the Ultimate Business Summit.)

He attributes a significant part of his business success to specifically addressing the negative issues that create disconnections with customers. After every home visit by a chimney sweep from one of his companies, a preaddressed and prestamped "How Did We Do?" postcard is left for the homeowner. It specifically asks them to identify the issues where the customer might believe the performance of the chimney sweep fell short of the promise that they perceive Ashbusters made.

As they say on cheesy infomercials—but wait! There's *more!*

The day after a technician from Ashbusters performs the scheduled service in your home, you'll receive a personal phone call from them to inquire—*again*—if there were any issues or problems. It isn't enough for Ashbusters to have satisfied customers. They want to be certain that Ashbusters has delivered an Ultimate Customer Experience. They are defensively pessimistic to make certain they do it exactly right for every customer, every time.

This may be a bigger task than you might imagine. According to Stoner, "We service about two to three hundred customers a week." That means they make up to sixty phone calls every day from their Nashville office. "It's a lot of work," Stoner said, "but we feel it's absolutely necessary."

Stoner's website, MarkStoner.com, states a similar philosophy. "By studying his failures . . . remaining focused and dedicated, and continuously striving to improve and learn, Mark has gone from *being owned* by his business to *owning* his business."

LET'S DISRUPT OURSELVES

How do individuals, patients, and consumers want their health care delivered, and what is the expectation they place on anybody that's delivering health care? That is the core question that the leadership team at St. Vincent Health Care in central Indiana started asking. It's their version of "what's pissing off our constituencies about health care?"

The result? Instead of focusing on expanding their huge campuses, St. Vincent is introducing several small regional facilities to be closer to patients and families. St. Vincent is looking to proactively deal with the rising pharmaceutical costs that are hurting their customers, as well as with the challenges presented by changes to care delivery. In addition, they promise to dramatically enhance the level of consumer education regarding health care issues available in their marketplace.

St. Vincent CEO Jonathan Nalli said, "We feel that if we don't drive transformation in health care, we will be disrupted and so we believe *disrupting ourselves* is the most important way to evolve health care as an industry."[54]

If you fail to focus on what is infuriating your customers, you can easily ignore the dissatisfaction that is the genesis of disruption.

HOW TO GO NEGATIVE

Your three action steps are to:

1. Probe internally for areas of weakness—and do it constantly. *Don't view talking about organizational or procedural weaknesses as a sign of negativity or weakness in the employee discussing it. Don't "shoot the messenger!" Learn from the message.*
2. Aggressively seek negative input from customers. *Find out what pisses them off! Then, fix it!*
3. Become "defensively pessimistic." *Examine in detail everything that could go wrong in every point of contact with customers. You can't fix what's broken if you aren't actively trying to discover what's damaged.*

Tesla cofounder Elon Musk supports this approach as well. "Pay attention to negative feedback and solicit it, particularly from friends," Musk said. "This may sound like simple advice, but *hardly anyone does that*, and it's incredibly helpful."[55]

Add the aforementioned founder of Amazon to this group. The richest person in the world provides customers with his email address so he can always be watching for the negative.

"In his book *The Everything Store*, author Brad Stone recounts the reaction Jeff Bezos sometimes has when a customer emails him at jeff@amazon.com to complain. Namely, he forwards the message to his leadership team 'with a one-character addition: a question mark,'" reports Bill Murphy, Jr. on Inc.com.

"Getting a question mark email is 'a ticking bomb' that 'elicits waves of panic,' according to Stone, as Amazon employees scramble to explain what went wrong—and make it right." [56]

However, as mentioned earlier, customers don't want you to have to "make it right."

Customers want you to GET it right.

Iconic companies and leaders are confident and self-assured enough to go negative. They obsess over learning what is pissing off their customers in order to ensure they will develop what it takes to get it right for them.

However, the willingness to go negative to serve customers does not mean you have a negative approach to the culture of your business. That's the point we will explore in the next chapter.

QUESTIONS FOR CHAPTER 6

- Have you done a SWOT analysis for your team, department, organization? If not, why not? If yes, did you experience the phenomenon when identifying "weaknesses" that were discussed in this chapter?

- Are your colleagues afraid to talk about how they couldn't discuss weaknesses—because it will be perceived as a weakness? (You need to have a conversation about this!)

- Do you welcome—or resist—discussions about negative aspects with your colleagues?

- Why would a customer recommend you to their friends or colleagues? What aspect of your organization (or team or department) do you want customers to be talking about to friends? (Product? Service? Brand?) How does your performance earn their referrals?

- Think about your approach. Is it:

    1. Self-handicapping?
    2. Strategically optimistic?
    3. Defensively pessimistic?

- What do you need to change to get your thinking (organizationally and individually) where you want it to be?

- And, finally: what pisses off your customers about doing business with you? What are you going to do about it?

CHAPTER SEVEN

#5 RECIPROCAL RESPECT

As my first wife and I were opening our wedding gifts many years ago, one stood out from the rest because of its uniqueness. It wasn't dishes or pots and pans—although starting our young lives together we were pleased with those too. Friends had gifted us with two tickets to see comedian Rodney Dangerfield. Our friends understood—quite correctly—that after the bustle of the marriage ceremony and reception and the time unpacking in our new apartment after our modest honeymoon in Gatlinburg, Tennessee, we would need a respite. Joining them for a night of laughter was just the thing we needed.

Rodney Dangerfield was a stand-up performer and actor who was a dominant force in the comedy scene in the 1980s and 90s. He won a Grammy for one of his comedy albums and starred in several films. He appeared on the *Tonight Show* over thirty times and sold out concert halls across the United States. It was just a year after Dangerfield's performance in the monster hit movie *Caddyshack*—perhaps the very height of his fame—and as we entered for the show, the theater was packed.

When Dangerfield walked on stage in his trademark black suit, white shirt, and red tie, the audience erupted in applause. He told a few great jokes for several minutes before he finally delivered his catchphrase all his fans were anticipating: "I get no respect—*no respect at all.*"

Oddly, later in the show, a man walked onto the stage carrying a pen and the program that was sold at the event. As Dangerfield was focused on his performance, the man walked almost up to his side. Dangerfield recoiled and shouted, "Get the hell off the stage!" The audience, assuming this was part of the show, laughed uproariously. Dangerfield shouted, "Where the hell is security in this dump?" At that point, three uniformed officers sprinted onto the stage, grabbed the man, and hauled him away. Still assuming this was all in the routine, the audience kept laughing—until it was obvious Dangerfield was very upset.

"Wow!" Sheri said as we strolled back to the car. "I can't believe that idiot just walked on stage and expected to get an autograph." She then thought for a moment and said, "I guess Rodney Dangerfield really *doesn't* get any respect!"

The Formerly
Terrific Employee

"Ever had an incredible employee and thought, *This is the one!* They were smart, engaged, driven, and seemed to really love the job. You thought, *We're going to be together forever!* You could really see yourself promoting this person, mentoring them, watching them climb the ranks in your company...and then one day, they quit. They might give you the 'It's not you, it's me' speech, but what does it actually mean?" asks author and speaker Bernard Marr on CNBC.com.

"*No respect*" is how Marr answers his question. "There's an old saying that employees don't leave a company, they leave a manager. No matter how much you like, respect, or appreciate an employee, if they don't know it, they may leave. Make sure your interactions with employees are always respectful, and that you look for ways to actively value their contribution."[57]

According to a study by Christine Porath, professor at the McDonough School of Business, and Christine Pearson of the Thunderbird School of Global Management, more people than ever are feeling disrespected at work. "Of the nearly 800 managers and employees across 17 industries [we] polled, those who didn't feel respected performed worse."

How much worse? The study indicated:

- 47 percent of those who were treated poorly intentionally decreased the time spent at work.
- 38 percent said they deliberately decreased the quality of their work.
- 66 percent reported their performance declined.
- 78 percent said their commitment to the organization had declined.[58]

You can't build an iconic organization or become an iconic leader when the productivity of your team is declining.

Leaders in any organization need to be aware of how their people are treated. A full 12 percent of those treated poorly said they "left their job because of the uncivil treatment. Yet, those who quit in response to incivility typically *don't tell their employers why*. When employees are exposed to rudeness, they are three times less likely to help others and their willingness to share drops by more than half."[59]

When your team feels respected by leadership, the research clearly shows they perform better. How much better?

- 92 percent greater focus and prioritization
- 55 percent more engagement

- 56 percent better health and well-being
- 89 percent greater enjoyment and satisfaction with their jobs.
- 1.72 times more trust and safety
- 1.1 times more likely to stay with their organizations than those who didn't[60]

How do you stand out from—and defeat—a competitor that has a team with 92 percent greater focus and 89 percent greater enjoyment and satisfaction with their jobs?

You *can't.*

Disrespected employees, as you might imagine, create an additional problem. They, in turn, *disrespect your customers.*

TRICKLE-DOWN DISRESPECT

My wife Tammy and I recently took a trip to Maui, adding a few days of vacation between two speeches I was presenting on the island. When we checked into our hotel room, a room service tray evidently from the previous occupants of our room sat in the hallway. A part of our shower was broken. A lightbulb in the bathroom was out. A sign at one elevator in the lobby was broken and had what appeared to be exposed wiring sticking out. Housekeeping made our bed each day, but the room wasn't really cared for. The ironing board remained out and trash remained in the can.

On our first day at the resort, I accidently left my key in the room and walked to the front desk to ask for another. I gently reminded the desk clerk to be certain that I also had access to the Regency Club, for which I qualified.

"No, you don't," she loudly stated. "It's nowhere on your record that you have access."

I softly explained I had the gold sticker on my key, had already been to the club, and was an elite member of their points program.

"No," she argued. "It's nowhere in here that you qualify."

"Well," I asked as politely as I could, stumbling for some kind of satisfactory resolution, "then how do I know about the gold sticker on the key?"

"You must have seen someone else's," she replied with obvious disdain.

Here's my question: even if I don't qualify, why be so disrespectful to a customer? Why not give the customer the benefit of the doubt? The biggest downside is that you would be out perhaps a couple cups of coffee and some slices of pineapple.

I returned to my room, found my original key with the gold sticker, and—for the heck of it—went back to the front desk. I simply said, "I wanted you to see this so you wouldn't think I was being dishonest with you."

Believe it or not, her response was, "Well, I have no idea how *you* got *that*!"

The next morning at the Maui resort, I put laundry in the bag the hotel provided and delivered it to the bell desk. Rather than greeting me with a "Good morning" or "How may I assist you?" instead the woman at the desk blurted out, "We normally come to the room and pick that up."

Oh," I responded with a smile. "Well, I saved you the trip then." Her response? "Harrumph."

No "Thank you" or "You shouldn't have" or "I'm calling security on you!" Nothing but "Harrumph."

After we returned home, I received a call from Hertz asking when I was planning on returning my Maui rental car to their location. My problem was that as we were checking out of the hotel, the Hertz desk there was unexpectedly closed. I asked the bellman who was carrying our luggage to the airport shuttle if he would help return the keys to the Hertz desk for me. He told me he would take care of it and I tipped him for his trouble. Somehow the car was never returned. Hertz was holding me responsible, which, of course, is what you would expect them to do. They didn't have their car!

When I called the hotel and asked for the bell desk, wouldn't you know it, I got Harrumph Lady. When I explained that a bell captain said he would take care of our rental car, she jumped in and said, "That cannot be true. We don't have bell captains working at that hour!"

"You don't have bellmen working at that hour?" I asked. "Then who helped me with my luggage?"

"We have bellmen, but there are no bell *captains* on duty then!" Rather than debate with her about the relative titles of members of the hotel bell staff, I hung up and called the Hertz desk at the resort.

Finally, I was treated as a customer should be. The agent promised to figure out what was wrong—and make it right. Not long after that, he called me back. He hadn't found the car or the keys, but he just wanted me to know that he was still working on it. An hour later, he called with the good news. He found the car. The bellman (who isn't a "captain," evidently) for some reason had moved the car to the wrong spot—and had forgotten to return the keys. Since the matter was not my fault, Hertz didn't charge me for the extra days. That difference in experience is precisely why I always rent from Hertz—and have never returned to that Maui resort.

A lot can be learned from this unusual customer service story.

When a customer receives such consistently disrespectful engagement at all levels—front desk, bell desk, bellman, for example—what is your guess about how the employees at that resort are being treated by their respective managers? How are those managers being respected by the general manager or CEO of their hotel? I think we all know the answer to that.

Think back to the story about Jack Miller and the Fairmont Scottsdale Princess. Do you imagine he consistently displays respect for his team? The Scottsdale Princess has among the lowest employee turnover rates of any hotel or resort in the world. That is not a coincidence.

RESPECT MUST BE EARNED

At a job I landed right out of college, my new boss told me about all of the people who had previously worked under him. He proudly related the professional success that they went on to achieve. As this was the first major-market radio station where I had ever worked, I was inspired by the long list of legendary broadcasters—and their achievements were my goals.

Not long after working there, I realized that I was employed by a manager who was a screamer. Regardless of the severity of your error—or even if he only *thought* you might have made one—he would explode with loud, outrageous, demeaning profanity.

Previously, my experience was with bosses who set high standards and aggressively held you to them. I had certainly worked for people who were a bit prickly and difficult. This, however, was my first experience working for someone who displayed no respect for his team.

After working there a year, I marched in his office and told him, "I quit."

"I get it," he said, "you aren't under contract here and another station offered you a better deal. What does it take to keep you?"

"That's not it at all," I replied. "I can't work like this. I just can't be productive when I'm treated the way you're treating me."

"Yeah, right. How much?" He assumed it was all a ploy to get a raise. That's how little respect he had.

Later, I found out that of the impressive list of successful broadcasters he touted on my first day, all of them had quit because of his disrespect. Without exception, they found employment somewhere they were treated with dignity, which allowed their careers to blossom, as they became nationally recognized professionals. Rather than being their launchpad, that screaming boss had been an anchor to their careers they had finally escaped.

Employees and customers are constantly—both consciously and subconsciously—evaluating the level of respect that is displayed towards them. Respect, as with being iconic, isn't something you achieve through demands. It must be *earned*.

Iconic leaders and organizations understand it is their responsibility to lead by example.

The iconic company or leader does not give respect only *after* respect is shown. They must show respect first. You can't grow plants without seed and sunshine coming first. You can't grow people without investing respect in them first.

The Key Is *Reciprocal* Respect

Iconic companies have cultures of uplifting reciprocal respect.
You may be a bit surprised to learn the single most important word in that sentence is *reciprocal*.

The word *reciprocal* dates back to the 1560s and comes from the Latin word *reciprocus*, which essentially means "returning *in the same way.*" In other words, reciprocal respect means that I will respect you in the same manner—and at the same level—as you display your respect for me.

"Professionals attract other professionals," Craig Huse of St. Elmo's Steakhouse in Indianapolis told me. "The people at St. Elmo have kept us successful and relevant through their passion for the restaurant. They are professionals doing something that most people treat simply as a job instead of a career. That's why many of our staff members have been with us twenty or more years." St. Elmo's has incredible employee retention and productivity because professionals who treat each other with respect attract other professionals who deserve and display the same.

This means that to develop iconic status, there are two particular aspects required for success:

1. How you display respect to others
2. Your unequivocal demand for respect at all levels

1) HOW YOU DISPLAY RESPECT TO OTHERS

After a decade of experience as a movie reviewer and commentator on the entertainment industry—and meeting more celebrities than you could imagine—there was one aspect that always left me befuddled: autographs. While I can understand why a fan would want a picture with a celebrity, I've never understood how getting them to sign on a piece of paper would thrill anyone. What I comprehend even less is why some stars refuse to do it.

In numerous situations, I've seen stars who refuse to sign anything or take pictures with their fans. This seems silly to me. The fan is responsible for your career. All of us should realize that we are beholden to our customers. If you're in show business and have no fans, we call you a waiter. I understand that some performers in show business are natural introverts—hiding behind a character or with a band and a song—and are reticent about personal engagement. But you can still be respectful and provide some "customer service." What I don't understand are the celebrities who are just jerks, pompously taking the time to condescendingly explain that they don't sign anything or ever take photos. The oddest part of this is that it takes them as long—or longer—to deliver the refusal than it would to just let their fan take the damn selfie.

In both cases, they deliver a degree of disrespect to their fans, or customers, that I find discouraging.

The nicest celebrities that I've ever been around?

- Arnold Schwarzenegger not only was engaging, he has booked me for presentations, including one at the White House with the president in the audience.
- Tom Hanks practically refused to talk about himself. Instead he enthusiastically praised others he had worked with on a project.
- My interview with Meryl Streep was delayed, so she asked if I'd like to go for coffee. We laughed and talked about our mutual connection to Indianapolis (her husband's hometown and my home for many years).
- John Travolta was late for his next appointment because we couldn't stop talking about men's suits. The next time we crossed paths, he

started with, "So, what designer am I wearing now?" With all the people that he meets—and as important as he is—I could not believe he remembered.

- The Oak Ridge Boys have been close friends for decades, and we still slip away from their concert halls to dine together several times a year.

Please don't read this and think it is an exercise in name-dropping! I'm not trying to impress you. I'm trying to express something important.

It's not that Schwarzenegger, Hanks, Streep, Travolta, and the Oaks became really popular and then said, "Well, we'd better start treating folks right, now that we're famous!" It's exactly the opposite. They displayed their respect first—and more studios, producers, concert promoters, fans, and journalists wanted to be associated with them.

How do you display respect to others? Most of this will—hopefully—come naturally to you. However, a simple reminder from time to time can be helpful.

SIX STEPS TO BECOMING RESPECTFUL

1. Don't just hear—listen
2. Display open body language
3. Don't nitpick

4. Show how you're following up
5. Don't withhold praise
6. Treat others equally and with sensitivity

Don't Just Hear—*Listen*

Hearing means you have the physical ability to turn the sounds expressed by others into meaningful language in your brain. *Listening* is a function of attention, the effort of taking the language and interpreting its deeper meaning. In a world with a myriad of distractions, focusing your attention and making the effort to hear customers and colleagues is a fundamental aspect of leadership.

Display Open Body Language

You can be taking in every word that I'm saying, but if your hands are on your hips or if your eyes roll toward the heavens, there's no script you can recite that will make me believe that you care. We all have sensors that tip us off as to whether or not someone is truly engaged. Your stance, your demeanor, and your tone of voice all register on our internal detection devices. Display openness in all you do—not just with the words you say.

Don't Nitpick

Have you ever worked with someone or been a customer dealing with an employee who argues about everything? If you said, "The sky is blue," they would disagree. "Haven't you been outside today?" these types might say. "The sky is gray! What the heck is wrong with you?" It seems as though they are waiting to correct something—anything. Does anyone ever want to be around these people? If you're always judging, criticizing, and dismissing others, they will eventually come to see you as a bully. We may believe we are merely offering "constructive criticism," but I challenge you. The next time you want to criticize or argue, ask yourself:

- Is it really "constructive"? Does it serve to help them or to make me appear as the authority?
- Do they desire the criticism? If they haven't invited your critique, then—from their viewpoint—all you are doing is bitching.

Show How You Are Following Up

After we have identified a problem, we are constantly told by everyone from our vendors to our kids that they will "get right on that." In many cases, we know that their comment is precisely where their effort ends.

It's a great sign of respect that you inform employees and customers that you will follow up. It's even more impressive when you demonstrate it. For example, notice how the Hertz employee picked up the phone and called to keep me posted. That's not only great customer service, it's a display of respect for the concern I was experiencing—worrying that the car had perhaps been stolen and I was going to be responsible. The follow-up was highly valued and appreciated by me, the customer. Every employee, every leader, and every organization can follow that model of respect.

DON'T WITHHOLD PRAISE

Here's another aspect that I personally find baffling. I know some people who act as though there is a limited supply of praise that they are granted to disseminate in their lifetime. They seem to hang onto it for fear that they'll exhaust their allocation. Or they might have other excuses like, "If I'm always praising my employees, they'll ask for a raise" or "If I keep telling them how good they are, they'll get a 'big head' and take it for granted." You know the routine.

Maybe they actually believe these inane ideas. Or maybe they aren't receiving enough praise themselves, so they refuse to provide it to others. Either way, it's never good to withhold validation from deserving customers or employees.

If you are not a millennial, it's even more important for you to understand why this aspect is so critical in achieving iconic status. Only 19 percent of millennial workers say they receive routine feedback at work, according to a study by Gallup. However, only 15 percent of millennials strongly agree that they *ask* for feedback they desire. "Millennials who meet with their manager on a regular basis are more than twice as likely as their generational peers to be engaged at work."[61]

Remember: you go first.

> *Millennials often aren't requesting your feedback. But they are silently hoping that you'll go first.*

TREAT OTHERS EQUALLY
AND WITH SENSITIVITY

It's terribly sad to me that anyone needs to be reminded of this—yet, perhaps all of us do.

I'd like to believe that no one ever goes to work thinking, *Today, I get to treat my team unequally and be insensitive to the needs of my customers!* Yet we probably have all observed that kind of behavior.

Hopefully, none of us would say that we want to pay women less than men for the same job or behave boorishly when it comes to our words and deeds toward other races, religions, and cultures. However, we know it happens.

Equality and respect are woven into the fabric of the conduct and performance of iconic organizations and leaders. Period.

I also would hope that as individuals and organizations become more enlightened, those who are being proactive and truly trying to change are not given a "death sentence" because of past missteps. Don't misunderstand—I'm not suggesting that they should be instantly forgiven for all misdeeds either. (And we also know that some will sprint to the altar because they know they're about to be caught.)

What I am suggesting is that if there is no path to recovery, there's no incentive for wrongdoers to quell the problem. All of us who desire change in the workplace also have to be willing to allow space for people who sincerely want to correct what they've done wrong. It's often said that the only people who dislike smoking worse than nonsmokers are former smokers. Could this be true of formerly disrespectful people as well? Might it be possible that if offenders can see both the damage and the opportunity, they can become more forceful advocates for change? I hope so.

Just as in the teachings of my chosen faith, forgiveness is only possible through salvation. But if there was no chance to be forgiven, what is the incentive to seek redemption?

Start today. Follow up on *all* six steps.

---

2) Do Not Tolerate Disrespect

Disrespect is like a weed in a garden. You've got to *kill it* or it will multiply and take over.

Your organization does not have to be arrogant, and you don't have to be an ass. Expecting to be treated respectfully when you are being respectful is neither haughty nor contemptible.

A contractor friend of mine in northern California has shared all kinds of stories on the rich and famous in the exclusive area where his business is located. After he worked on remodeling a superstar's home, he told me one I'll never forget.

This superstar also owned a very exclusive country club. A multimillionaire businessman had just joined the club. On his first round, he played exceedingly slow and left his trash on the course for others to pick up. He was behaving contemptibly. To top it off, when he came into the clubhouse after playing golf, he was rude to the server.

Just then the superstar owner of the country club appeared holding a check made out to the member. It was the refund of his large initiation fee.

"We don't tolerate disrespect here," the iconic figure told the millionaire. "Our team members are as important as our club members. You're no longer welcome on the property."

I'm certain every single employee of that country club in northern California would agree their superstar boss had just "made their day."

While that's a good story, it's also an instructive lesson. The iconic entertainer didn't merely tell everyone how much he respected them—he demonstrated it. And how do you suppose the other members of the club now act toward the employees—and other club members as well?

The superstar owner killed the weeds of disrespect before they could take over.

DISRESPECTFUL BEHAVIOR SHOULD NEVER BE TOLERATED

An aforementioned friend—author and hall of fame speaker, Larry Winget—frequently talks about the importance of respect. He inspired me to make a list of the seven disrespectful behaviors that I won't tolerate. Your list may be different—here's mine:

1. *Dishonesty.* If I know you'll lie to me, what can you say or do that I can possibly believe?
2. *Disloyalty.* A variation of dishonesty. It's a betrayal of the trust that I've placed in someone.
3. *Apathy.* If we actively disagree, that's fine. It's hard to respect someone who just doesn't give a damn about anything.

4. *Stratification.* This is someone who respects people differently. They may be courteous to a colleague and mean to a waiter. You know the type—someone who will kiss up to the boss and kick anyone below them on the org chart. Disgusting.

5. *Selfishness.* It's not all about you—and it's certainly not all about me. If you can't recognize that, I don't want me to be around you.

6. *Inequality.* If you think that your gender is better, your race is preferred, and there are people lesser than you, we're done.

7. *Totalism.* That's the word I use to describe people who think their side is totally right—and those with other viewpoints are totally wrong. This is what has led to the lack of significant discussion and meaningful conversation on important issues in every nation around the world.

What if your organization made its own list of seven disrespectful behaviors that you won't tolerate and posted them prominently? How would that shape the behavior of your team—and your customers?

- The employees you want to attract will not work where they aren't respected. Therefore, aside from just being the right thing to do, it makes great economic sense to be respectful to them.

• The customers you want to attract aren't going to do business where they aren't shown respect. Therefore, aside from just being the right thing to do, it makes great economic sense to prove your respect for them.

As I mentioned in chapter 3, there are many annual lists touting the results of studies on the best places to work.

Fortune, for example, listed their top five in 2018 as Salesforce, Wegman's, Ultimate Software, Boston Consulting Group, and Edward Jones.[62] Glassdoor listed Facebook, Bain & Company, Boston Consulting Group (again), In-N-Out Burger, and Google.[63]

It should not escape our attention that these are all remarkably successful corporations. While some might suggest that it's easier for winning companies to treat their people right, I'd advocate that it's *because* they are treating their teams with reciprocal respect that they are so successful.

Note, too, that these companies do everything from serving burgers to offering financial services—from consulting major corporations to bagging groceries. There is no thread that unites them other than they are all great places to work. It's impossible to receive this extraordinary level of positive reviews from your employees without reciprocal respect.

- 95 percent of Salesforce employees agree that "people care about each other here."
- 96 percent advocate that "management is honest and ethical in its business practices."
- 48 percent of the reporting employees at Salesforce are millennials, 44 percent gen Xers, and just 8 percent are baby boomers.[64]

Wegman's Food Markets—where the job descriptions are highly different and baby boomers make up almost three times more of the workforce than they do at Salesforce—reports almost identical responses about their organization.[65] In other words it's not about the industry, or the job, or the employee's generation. It's about the reciprocal respect in the organization.

FIRE THEM!

If you have someone on the team who doesn't respect his colleagues: *Fire them.*

If you have someone in your organization who won't respect her customers: *Fire them.*

If you have a customer who will not respect your employees: **Fire them, too.**

"Everyone deserves respect, but some clients think that rule doesn't apply to them. In a distorted sense of reality, some clients believe they can treat you like dirt because they are paying you," says Nathan Gotch, founder of Gotch SEO. "Think about it this way . . . would you continue being friends with someone who was rude or disrespectful? Probably not."

"So," Gotch continues, "why would you take that type of abuse from a client? Money is nice, but your sanity is what matters. If your heart races when you think about your rude client, then it's time to make change."[66] I couldn't agree more.

Why would your best employees want to continue in your organization if they are expected to tolerate customers or clients who disrespect them? That's obviously not iconic behavior.

What you tolerate is what you endorse.

What you tolerate is what you endorse. In other words, when you tolerate disrespectful behavior from some customers, you endorse that behavior in other customers too. The discourteous actions you fail to stop with one employee become the actions you have just endorsed among all employees. By not stopping the disrespectfulness immediately and boldly, you are saying that you approve the behavior. It's all-inclusive. If you allow one person to do it, you are really saying that you're allowing others to do so as well.

My pal Larry Winget suggested I change the word *tolerate* to *endorse* when I speak on respect. I now pass that advice on to my clients.

Try it! When you're talking about a specific employee or customer's attitudes or behaviors, just change the word *tolerate* to *endorse*. It may change your perspective. For example, I can almost hear discussions that may have taken place about men who were making unwanted advances on women in the workplace. Somewhere, someone may have said that because of the man's position, power, reputation, sales success, or other achievements, the company would "have to tolerate" some of his bad behavior.

Some insiders—"off the record," of course—confessed that Miramax Films had "tolerated" Harvey Weinstein's behavior because of his status and track record. What if, instead, it was required that the board or other senior officers had to publicly announce that they had "endorsed" his repulsive actions? Could you imagine that? Absolutely not!

Once we switch the word *tolerate* to *endorse*, our perspective on bad behavior becomes better focused.

ICONIC LEVELS OF RESPECT

If you want to obtain, maintain, or regain iconic status, it's not going to be accomplished in a vacuum. You'll need a team of customers and employees who advocate for you in today's connected marketplace.

This can only happen when you extend to others the respect you desire for yourself and your organization. You must refuse to tolerate disrespect from those who are missing the confidence to engage without vitriol or unacceptable behavior.

You cannot grow your garden unless you're willing to kill the weeds.

Endorse the behavior you desire. Extend—and expect to obtain—high levels of respect from all. You're not Rodney Dangerfield. You can get—and give—respect. It's just part of who iconic people *are,* and what iconic people *do.*

THE FIVE FACTORS OF ICONIC PERFORMANCE

There you have it. Those are the five factors of an iconic performance:

1. Play Offense
2. Get Promise and Performance Right

3. Stop Selling
4. Go Negative
5. Reciprocal Respect

Our next important question is this: what happens when you've attained iconic status, have maintained it for a period of time, then lose it?

Can you ever get it back? Can you ever return to the highest level of distinction?

That's what we'll examine in our next chapter.

Questions for Chapter 7

- When do you feel like Rodney Dangerfield—and you get "no respect"? What do you do about it?
- How would you rate the level of respect that your organization delivers to your employees?
- How would you evaluate the level of respect that your colleagues share with you? What can you do to make the answers to both of these two previous questions even greater?
- How do you demonstrate that you are REALLY listening?
- Strike the pose! How would you stand (or sit) to display open body language?
- Are you a "nitpicker"? How could you respond to one in a manner that helps them?
- How do you demonstrate that you're following up?
- Name the last three times you praised someone—and the compliment wasn't coupled with anything negative!
- When have you failed to be treated with dignity?
- How can you make certain no one you come in contact with feels that way?
- What actions from others have you "tolerated" that you would not "endorse"?
- What are you going to do to stop tolerating/endorsing such behavior?

PART THREE

BRINGING IT
ALL TOGETHER

CHAPTER EIGHT

REGAINING ICONIC STATUS

If you remember at the very beginning of the book I mentioned a few market leaders in decline or no longer in existence: Sears, Nokia, HoJo's. We could add many more companies to our list:

> Compaq, EF Hutton, Woolworth's (the US company), Arthur Andersen, TWA, Blockbuster, B. Dalton's Booksellers, Kodak, Service Merchandise, MCI WorldCom, Golfsmith, Radio Shack, Toys "R" Us, Western Auto, Tower Records, Circuit City, PanAm, Casual Corner, Bethlehem Steel, Lehman Brothers, Levitz Furniture, Border's Bookstores, Oldsmobile, Sports Authority, Mervyn's, Crazy Eddie's, Linens 'n Things, Dominick's, Waldenbooks, FAO Schwartz

You could probably name *many* more.

The question: if you lose your iconic status, can it ever be regained?

The answer is: it depends.

There are three critical factors that determine whether or not you can regain iconic status:

1. Where you are in your slide
2. Why the slide occurred
3. How the market perceives you now

WHERE YOU ARE IN YOUR SLIDE

Obviously, there is a point of no return. Maybe you're overleveraged and you cannot finance your future obligations. Or maybe some new technology has made you irrelevant and obsolete. For some, if you discover you are on the slide early enough, you still have time to prevent extinction.

"At Wells Fargo, CEO Tim Sloan admitted the bank had been slow to adapt to a changing financial landscape. 'Five years ago, we were the most valuable financial institution in the world,' said Sloan, before pointing out that the bank suffered some complacency. 'That will never again happen at Wells Fargo.. . . You can't rest on your laurels as much as we did.'"[67]

For example, why did companies like Spotify eventually destroy companies like Tower Records? Obviously, downloading tracks—like we did legally on iTunes or not so legally from other services—replaced buying CDs. Now, streaming music has replaced downloading tracks. So why didn't Tower do that first—or at all? They already possessed significant resources and industry relationships. It certainly wasn't that we all stopped loving our music. The answer, to a great degree, is that by the time complacent Tower Records realized the marketplace and the desired delivery method had changed, it was too late. They were in the wrong business.

You've probably heard the stories of Netflix trying to sell their company to Blockbuster and the Wright Brothers attempting to get Union Pacific to acquire their patents on flight. The reason Blockbuster and Union Pacific didn't see the opportunity before them is because they were thinking small—about their specific business, but not the larger opportunities in their industry.

- Blockbuster thought they were in the retail business, *not the entertainment distribution industry.*
- Union Pacific thought they were in the railroad business, *not the transportation industry.*
- Tower Records thought they were in the album or CD retail sales business, *not the music distribution industry.*

By the time these companies recognized they were on the road to oblivion, it was too late to reestablish their distinctive status. Let's face it, everything goes faster when it's heading downhill.

If you're losing your iconic status, you must be brutally honest about where you are on the descending slide.

WHY THE SLIDE OCCURRED

The primary reason why a company's reputation and market share is sliding provides insight into whether or not the company will return to iconic—or even distinctive—status.

If your company is sliding because of ethical reasons, there is likely little hope of regaining iconic status. It is much easier to destroy a reputation than it is to rebuild one. Take Enron for example. It was a behemoth energy company in the late 1990s that got into the derivatives market trading all sorts of commodities, some of which did poorly. Enron hid its losses for as long as it could, but eventually it was found out. And when it was, all hell broke loose. The company went down and caused the demise of famed accounting firm Arthur Andersen along with it.

And remember Theranos, the biotech company I mentioned in chapter 4 that lied about contracts with the Department of Defense to boost its credibility? Would you ever again believe anything Theranos claimed? When unethical behavior is behind your decline, your goose is likely cooked.

Yet, for most, the slide occurs not because of deceit but myopia.

The slide generally happens because of the narrow-minded, shortsighted approach that many entrepreneurs, corporate executives, and sales professionals take.

Such an approach creates a blindness toward the marketplace and a bias about their product or service that practically ensures poor decision making about the future.

The good news is that if your approach or mindset is your problem—as opposed to unethical behavior—there may be a chance of recovery. But you need to act quickly. You must be brutally honest as to why the slide occurred.

To stop the slide, you must be brutally honest as to why the slide occurred.

Stating, "We didn't do anything wrong" simply assures the marketplace that you aren't going to be the one to fix the problem.

HOW THE MARKETPLACE PERCEIVES YOU NOW

Do good feelings remain in the marketplace for you? Could it be reestablished and expanded?

Remember my story about Nokia in the introduction? Nokia may have been down, but they weren't out. There remained a vast reservoir of goodwill for Nokia. Their current resurgence as a technology and software company specializing in network solutions, as well as cloud, artificial intelligence, 5G mobility, and IoT (Internet of Things) services holds potential.

Nokia's reputation was still intact enough to make a comeback. However, I don't think a new version of Radio Shack, for example, would hold any appeal. They had their chance for years and didn't deliver in a compelling manner for customers when they had the opportunity to do so.

In other words, how you treat someone the first time is how they assume you will treat them again. If you lost out because of reasons other than poor service, you may have enough goodwill left in the tank to restart your organizational engine.

How do you regain Iconic status?

If, after review, you've determined that

- you can stop the slide before extinction,
- the slide occurred for correctable reasons, and
- enough goodwill remains in the marketplace for customer reengagement—then it's time to get started reclaiming your iconic status.

While there is much to do—and many prospective approaches that you could take—my research and experience suggests these three primary principles:

1. Think start-up
2. Work from the inside out
3. Build performance before enhancing promise

THINK START-UP

Would a start-up announce that they were going to be "all things to all people"? Of course not. Uber didn't begin by proclaiming that they were going to deliver meals and transport patients to health care appointments. They started by specifically focusing on the dissatisfaction people had with taxicabs.

> *To reclaim iconic status, you're going to need a more innovative mindset—you need to start thinking like a start-up.*

The goal of the start-up is not to maintain the status-quo. The start-up seeks to destroy those "way it's always been done" procedures.

When companies want to rebuild their status, many seem to desire to do so without significantly changing how they think and approach the market. Trying to reestablish your position in the marketplace by holding on to your old way of business is essentially blaming your customers for your decline. It's akin to saying to customers, "Obviously, you didn't 'get it' when we tried this before.

Now, we're giving you another chance to see how terrific we are."

It used to be that we accepted the philosophy in business that *"the big eat the small."* This meant that size was the strategic advantage in the marketplace.

It used to be *"the fast eat the slow"*—meaning that speed to market and rapidity of change were the primary factors.

However, once again, the rules have changed. Now, for lack of better terminology, it is that *"the smart eat the dumb* (or perhaps, the "less savvy").

In other words, to recover your iconic status you must be more

- perceptive about where customer dissatisfaction is based,
- insightful about the opportunity that provides, and
- shrewd in delivering on your promises.

This is what rules in today's market. This is why we often see the articles, books, and research on the methods and concepts of such brilliant start-up leaders as Gary Vaynerchuk (see chapter 5) and others like Leo Wildrich of Buffer, Jess Weiner of TTJ Consulting and Changemakers, Mark Cuban, Bert Jacobs of Life Is Good, and Julie Rice, cofounder of SoulCycle. It's not about their speed—it's about their smarts.

> Don't start by asking how you reestablish your current franchise. Ask how a start-up would erase the dissatisfaction that your customers face.

If you're having challenges coming up with the ideas and potential solutions you need, why not ask a start-up to assist? Tim Sloan, CEO of Wells Fargo, admitted at a conference that is exactly what the financial giant has done when it comes to making it easier for customers to get mortgages processed more efficiently. When Sloan realized Wells Fargo couldn't design the product itself, "it turned to Blend, a San Francisco startup, for help."[68]

Work from the Inside-Out

No amount of television spots or online ads can overcome a negative internal culture. Yet, unfortunately, many companies that have an internal issue will launch outward efforts to recover iconic status. Until your culture is right *internally*—no matter the size of your organization—many of your external efforts won't help. Instead, they'll just draw more attention to your dysfunction and help speed your demise.

Until your culture is right internally,
many of your external efforts won't
help.

For example, United Airlines is a client of mine and I'm a Global Services member of their MileagePlus frequent flyer program. I have already put my tail in their seats for over one hundred thousand miles this year. I have great appreciation and respect for them. Unfortunately, because of several incidents that have attracted global attention, their reputation has been wounded. Until they get their internal culture better aligned and everyone on the same page to deliver a great customer experience, investing in a new "Fly the Friendly Skies" ad campaign is not going to help.

A strong internal culture is what enables your organization to align the promise-performance matrix we discussed in chapter 4. Deloitte is a $40-billion-dollar, multinational company specializing in audit, consulting, and tax services, among others. One of their executives in human capital, Anthony Abbatiello, defines *culture* as the "set of values and attributes that shape how things get done in the organization."[69] He proposes three steps to help align your culture with the strategy of your organization:

1. **Define who your culture carriers are.** These are often leaders. Define what leader behav-

iors need to be in order to live the culture. To increase courage, for example, leaders should support their staff when taking risks.

2. **Systematically reinforce the behavior.** Find important company events where culture comes out, such as sales process, annual budget process, and the performance management process. Rewarding or aligning those with attributes of behavior is important in monitoring culture.

3. **Have leaders tell stories.** "There's a power of storytelling in an organization that is really important for the culture and for connecting emotionally with your workforce," Abbatiello said. When communicating the importance of taking risks, employees will respond to a story about a risk the leader took, how they failed, and what they learned. This is more powerful than simply hearing a leader say, "Take risks."[70]

As a United customer, I wondered why they weren't taking quicker strides toward improving the customer experience. Then I realized—especially after seeing the awful video of the passenger being dragged off the plane in Chicago and reading of the death of a family pet in an overhead bin—the only way their management could make a change in the customer experience was to first change the internal culture. This is an effort that

1. takes significant time to successfully accomplish, and
2. is seldom readily apparent to those outside the organization.

After I had the opportunity to work for and with the airline—and meet several members of their senior leadership team—I walked away impressed by both their effort and the size of their task. Tens of thousands of United employees deliver the "friendly skies" experience every day. Yet, it is one gate agent in Chicago or a single flight attendant on a plane from Houston who makes headlines.

The flight attendant whom I saw comfort a scared little boy traveling as an unaccompanied minor—and the representative on the telephone who helps you—is privately appreciated. The one who is rude gets blasted on Trip Advisor and read about by thousands.

The challenge for every organization is that *every* team member needs to be on board with providing an excellent experience. In today's world of ubiquitous cameras and social media, all it takes is one single individual who does something wrong to garner you worldwide derision. Because iconic leaders understand this concept, there is *no excuse* for not pursuing the principles of reciprocal respect outlined in chapter 7 in order to achieve the goal of total employee engagement.

United's position, in my opinion, was diminished by a previous leadership team. Will they ever reclaim its iconic status as the "friendly skies" airline? There are no guarantees. However, I promise you that the current team, led by CEO Oscar Munoz, is working from the inside out—with enormous effort and grit—to make that happen.

Like United, the legacy telephone company in Australia (and client of mine), Telstra, has suffered from customer service challenges. One executive there told me that at one point Telstra's residential customer service was so inferior it was impacting sales in the corporate division and even their mobile telephone operations. Customers assumed if Telstra could not get their residential service right, why should they trust them with their mobile or business needs?

To combat these problems, Telstra's HR professionals worked with senior leaders to redevelop their vision and values. Working directly with the CEO, they recently articulated what "the desirable culture and values should be to establish a 'One Telstra' mindset and relevant behaviors towards customers."[71] Part of the beauty—and that's the right word—is that "One Telstra" recognizes that all components of the company have to be aligned internally before they can expect results externally.

It must happen throughout the organization!

"Turning customers into lifelong advocates requires companies to embrace the customer experience throughout the organization," Jason Bradshaw of Volkswagen Group Australia told me. "We've been working diligently to create a culture that embodies the following philosophy: *If I have a problem in front of me, my job is to get that problem fixed. If I have two problems, my priority is the problem that impacts our drivers and our owners.*"

Bradshaw is absolutely right.

BUILD PERFORMANCE BEFORE ENHANCING PROMISE

"Give us another chance!" sliding companies seem to be saying. "We will do better next time!"

But what if you *don't*?

If you are going to regain iconic status, it will happen because you have rebuilt a solid, dependable performance *before* you restate or enhance your promise to customers. Business relationships mirror personal relationships, and rebuilding trust with a customer is a lot like trying to regain the trust of a girlfriend or boyfriend. It takes a lot to be able to get a second chance—and a third or fourth chance is practically impossible.

If your company has fallen from its iconic status, there is a reason that customers have "broken up" with you. Getting them back is a monumental task because they assume if it didn't work out previously, it's not going to work out at all. At best you might get a mere second chance to reestablish any kind of positive relationship with your customer base. They have to see that you will do what you said you will do. You *must* deliver.

What tends to happen? Many organizations and leaders become so desperate to reengage, they make exaggerated claims in an attempt to capture the customer's attention—knowing that mindshare always precedes market share. However, you grow neither for the long run by making claims that cannot be supported. If you can't deliver on your promises, all you're doing is accelerating your descent into Fraud territory.

Volkswagen Group Australia is an example of how to do it right.

Given the well-publicized emissions scandal that Volkswagen faced recently, that statement may come as a bit of a surprise.

The leadership team for VW in Australia—led by Group Managing Director Michael Bartsch—has focused on what they can control. Over the past couple of years, resale values of the cars sold by Volkswagen Group Australia have not been impacted, suggesting that their efforts are successful. VW dealers in Australia remain more profitable than most. "The values of the vehicles reflect normal lifecycle and our dealerships are profitable," said Bartsch. "They're performing at a level above most franchises in Australia in terms of return on sales."[72]

This is not to suggest that VW Australia was immune to the challenges presented by the misdeeds of their corporate parent in Germany. However, the impact of this situation "down under" has been notably less than in the United States due to the strong initiative by the VW dealers in Australia to enhance the customer experience. When the scandal first hit, Chief Customer Officer Jason Bradshaw knew his team had to take action. Extensive training across all dealerships nationwide was not an easy sell because tangible results are challenging to quantify. Nevertheless, Bradshaw was determined to improve the customer experience.

The results of building performance first have been evident in VW Australia sales, growth in dealership profitability, and enthusiasm throughout the organization. It enabled VW Group Australia to go to market with the "Premium for the People" campaign discussed in chapter 5. "I think that's a real testament to how, as an organization, we want to be obsessed about continuous improvement and everyone taking accountability," Bradshaw told me.

If you are trying to regain iconic status, it won't be easy. Nothing in this chapter should be seen as a quick fix. You are facing difficult odds. Rebuilding trust with customers requires extraordinary effort and restoring the luster to an eroded brand takes immense perseverance.

However, what's the alternative?

There's no justification for giving up on formerly distinctive, iconic organizations that have faded from importance. Why wouldn't you fight to keep your status—or to reclaim your esteem in the marketplace?

In the final chapter, I'll close with some insight provided by an amazing restaurant—and with a challenge for you to reach the ultimate level of distinction.

QUESTIONS FOR CHAPTER 8

- Is your status in the marketplace on the rise or on the decline? If you're ascending, how do you sustain your growth? If you're declining, where are you currently located on the slide?
- Why has your marketplace position eroded? If it has not declined, identify a competitor that has and answer why they met that fate.
- Think like a start-up and come up with three "start-up" ideas for your business.
- What shifts, changes, additions, or subtractions need to be made to your organizational or departmental culture?
- Name a company that *talked* about how much better they had become but didn't deliver. How did that make you feel about them? Did you continue to do business with them?

CONCLUSION

YOU Can Become Iconic

To review, the Five Factors of Iconic Performance are:

1. **Play Offense**
2. **Get Promise and Performance Right**
3. **Stop Selling**
4. **Go Negative**
5. **Reciprocal Respect**

When you execute each of these five factors with excellence, you can move your organization—and your personal leadership abilities—from distinctive to iconic.

Although many of the examples of iconic companies in this book have been million-dollar businesses, you do not have to be big to be an iconic company. You don't have to be globally recognized like Mark Zuckerberg or Jeff Bezos to be an iconic leader. One example is an entrepreneur whose business is not iconic . . . yet.

THE VALET BREWER

On many occasions, I would pull my car to the valet stand at Green Valley Resort and Casino in Henderson, Nevada, to be greeted by a parking attendant whom I knew only as Dave.

After many occasions of friendly, generic small talk, Dave asked me what I did for a living. When I told him that I was an author of business books and professional speaker, he inquired if I had a podcast or other audio-books he might download. I told Dave about my pod-cast, "Project Distinct." In all candor, I thought this extremely nice guy was just being kind to a regular cus-tomer. The next time I parked at Green Valley, Dave rushed up and commented on a recent podcast. Wow! He really had been listening! Then, Dave told me his job was at Green Valley Ranch for a steady income and the benefits. His business, however, was owning and running a craft brewery in Las Vegas.

Dave Forrest and his wife, Wyndee, had the idea for starting up Craft Haus Brewery while on a trip together through Europe. What they wanted to bring back home—"one pint at a time," as Wyndee says—is not just European beer, but a European beer experience.

Dave invited Tammy and me to the brewery for a tour. I was a bit reticent, because I don't know anything about beer. (I'm more of a bourbon guy!)

However, Dave's engaging manner made it impossible to say no.

Before visiting, I was at a local supermarket and noticed Craft Haus beer being sold there. For the heck of it, I picked up a six-pack of their Belgard Coffee Stout, because at least I know I like coffee. Imagine my surprise to discover that I absolutely loved their brew.

We toured the brewery during their annual Comrade Day. Craft Haus will brew a special Russian Imperial Stout for sale only on that day. Then, they throw an all-day party at the brewery to enjoy this special batch of beer. During this visit, I met many customers who were passionate fans of Craft Haus.

Dave and Wyndee focus on creating an experience for their customers. The brewery holds everything from yoga classes that are combined with craft beer tasting to hosting a sausage and beer festival complete with a European food truck.

It is truly amazing! This little brewery is

- bringing high quality products to a marketplace ruled by beer giants like Budweiser and Miller Lite;
- producing innovative products, such as the stout beer brewed with an elite coffee blend;
- developing creative customer experiences—from Comrade Day to yoga in a brewery.

What business—of any size—couldn't learn from a company that is delivering innovative, quality products wrapped around a unique, Ultimate Customer Experience?

From humble beginnings to selling craft beer in supermarkets and at fine dining establishments, the valet parking attendant who owns a craft brewery is on his way to developing an iconic business.

THE IMPACT OF SMALL ICONIC COMPANIES

While the story of Dave and Wyndee might sound like a nice anecdote about young entrepreneurs, it's also illustrative of how small iconic businesses can impact global leaders.

Billionaire Jorge Paulo Lemann, cofounder of 3G Capital—which owns several global food and beverage conglomerates, such as AB InBev (which includes all of the Budweiser and Miller beer brands)—recently called himself a "terrified dinosaur."

"I've been living in this cozy world of old brands and big volumes," said Lemann. "We bought brands that we thought could last forever"—and borrowed cheap money to do so, according to a report in *Forbes*. He added: "You could just focus on being very efficient (in the past). All of a sudden we are being disrupted."

"Craft took us by surprise," Lemann confessed.

Certainly, Lemann and AB InBev will respond to the challenge. What else would we expect them to do? And they are responding in a manner similar to the points suggested in the previous chapter. AB InBev and Lemann's team created a new business—Zx Ventures—with the goal of investing in innovations like craft beer, e-commerce, and home brewing. Lemann described this as "self-disruption."

"We hope this will be a model which we can build on," he said. "I'm not going to lie down and go away."[73]

By leveraging their unique connection to their customers—and by using their savvy understanding of the marketplace—Craft Haus can survive and thrive no matter what the AB InBev team chooses to do. Dave and Wyndee are small business entrepreneurs who think like iconic leaders.

The Circle City Steak House

A smallish restaurant in a mid-sized city in the Midwest has proven you can go up against globally known competition and achieve iconic status.

Indianapolis, Indiana, has long been called the Circle City because the midpoint of the metropolis isn't a block like Times Square. Instead, the center of the city is Monument Circle.

In 1902, the Soldiers and Sailors Monument—a memorial 284.5 feet tall to honor Hoosiers who served in the Civil War—was dedicated in the middle of that circle. A few months later, Joe Stahr opened a tavern and buffet restaurant two blocks away and named it after the patron saint of sailors. He brought in a beautiful tiger-oak back-bar from Chicago. St. Elmo's was simply a small tavern with a standard menu. When the first Indianapolis 500 was held in 1911, St. Elmo's was already nine years old.

In 1946, Sam and Ike Roth purchased the restaurant and invited their brother Harry, who was an optometrist, to join them. Harry said he went from "eye glasses to bar glasses," and in 1956, when his brothers left the restaurant, Harry invited a lifelong friend, Isadore "Izzy" Rosen, to join him.

With Izzy's larger-than-life personality—a trait that served him well in his previous profession as a bookie—and Harry's quiet business skill, they made a terrific team. St. Elmo's became, according to their website, "a place where salesmen and tycoons came to seal the deal, where attorneys and politicians strategized and plotted, where coaches and players celebrated wins and lamented losses, where celebrities came to unwind from a show."[74]

It still is the place where those encounters occur in Indianapolis.

From 1947 to 1986, Harry and Izzy skillfully guided St. Elmo to continued success. They turned over the reins to veteran Indianapolis restauranteur Stephen Huse, who remains the present owner. In 1997, Huse partnered with his son, Craig, who is now the president of the corporation. Craig says his favorite quote is "A good restaurant serves its customers; a great restaurant entertains its guests."[75]

Local lore in Indianapolis has it that St. Elmo's is responsible for both a Super Bowl and a super concert.

The NFL holds its players combine—the event for scouting college players who are prospective pros—every year in Indianapolis. So many NFL owners, coaches, and executives loved dining at St. Elmo's during that event it helped Indianapolis secure that sport's championship game—one seen annually by a billion viewers around the world.

When the Rolling Stones were touring the United States a few years back, music industry veterans were surprised to see they were playing two consecutive nights in Indianapolis but only one show in much larger cities. Keith Richards is reported to have said the reason was they wanted to dine again a second night at St. Elmo's. (And they did!)

Celebrity appearances might be uncommon for most of the Midwest, but they're nothing new at St. Elmo's. The Wine Cellar Room is usually called the Peyton Manning Room because of his frequent visits there, even now that he's retired.

They also have a private dining area called the Card Room named in honor of Bon Jovi. "He and Cher dined with us many years ago and would play cards after their show," said Kirsten DeWitte, St. Elmo's private dining manager.[76]

Up on the second level of the restaurant is the private Huse Dining Room. Right outside the window is the iconic St. Elmo sign. Former Indiana governor and current United States Vice President Mike Pence often enjoys a good steak in the Huse Dining Room.

It's obvious St. Elmo's is a great place to eat in Indianapolis. *Forbes* named it one of the "10 Great Classic Restaurants Well Worth Visiting" in the world. And they've received the prestigious America's Classic award from the James Beard Foundation.

But what does this mean for your business?

Take a look at how St. Elmo's delivers on all Five Factors of Iconic Performance.

St. Elmo's *Plays Offense*

Morton's, Ruth's Chris, and Fleming's make up three of the eleven steakhouses within a few of blocks of each other, all downtown in the Circle City. Yet you cannot get Craig Huse or his team to talk much about them. It's not that they are uninformed about their competition; it's that they are playing offense and choose not to focus on their "faceless opponents."

"There are fourteen other steakhouses operating just in downtown Indianapolis," Huse told me. "We focus inside our four walls—as there will always be competitors. Each new opening reminds us that we have to delight our guests each and every time. We cannot ride the coattails of our successful past into the future."

ST. ELMO'S *GETS PROMISE AND PERFORMANCE RIGHT*

St. Elmo's makes a promise that is embodied in a comment from Craig Huse:

> Jim Nantz of CBS Sports, says that St. Elmo is his favorite restaurant in the world. Certainly, we are not the best restaurant in the world, but we are the best restaurant in Jim Nantz's world . . . and that is what we aspire to with each of our guests.

You can't be the favorite restaurant of such a well-traveled, experienced professional as iconic broadcaster Jim Nantz without *delivering exactly what you promise.*

Aspiring to be someone's favorite restaurant—and delivering the performance that's congruent with the promise—is a major element in what makes St. Elmo's iconic. And when your promise and performance are aligned in the right spot, customers can become your biggest advocates.

St. Elmo's leverages the willingness of their customers to recommend them through their Patron Saints program. "This recognizes some of our very best guests," Huse said. "These guests not only dine with us frequently, but they also have a sense of pride—they advocate for our restaurant to their friends, family, coworkers, and even the person sitting next to them on the airline."

Isn't it fascinating that this is not the typical loyalty program where points are accrued and exchanged for free meals? "A Patron Saint does not earn points or discounts because we don't want to devalue our relationship. We simply do the little things that prioritize these very special guests." Patron Saints have a special phone number for reservations, reserved table signs with their names on them, and "random acts of surprise and delight," as Huse put it. With that kind of recognition for guests, doesn't it make sense they would be vibrant advocates for St. Elmo's?

St. Elmo's *Stopped Selling*

When you visit Indianapolis, you may see reminders of the St. Elmo experience. However, you'll never see them hawking the restaurant in the manner that you'll observe from other local establishments and national chains in the city.

You don't become Jim Nantz's favorite restaurant, the place where Peyton Manning hangs out, where Jon Bon Jovi and Cher play cards, and the vice president enjoys a steak because you twisted their arms into coming and having dinner.

It's amazing that we've discussed St. Elmo's and I have yet to bring up their world-famous shrimp cocktail sauce! The amazing—and amazingly spicy, horseradish-laden—sauce is known around the world. It serves as a discussion point and conversation starter. Through this unique condiment, St. Elmo's has an element that engages customers. You might be asking: are younger professionals interested in a two-hour meal—typically with a hearty steak in the restaurant's main dining room? After researching that issue, they opened the "1933 Lounge" above their traditional restaurant to ensure continued relevancy in a changing market. "We don't want to become known as your grandfather's steakhouse."

Younger professionals "want small plates and craft cocktails in an atmosphere conducive to relaxation and conversation, within sightlines of the bar. We tried to make this area a sexy juxtaposition to the black-suited service in the dining rooms on our main level," Huse said.

When combined with superior food and extraordinary service, they don't have to sell...because they *attract* customers of all generations.

ST. ELMO'S *GOES NEGATIVE*

Craig Huse—following in the tradition of his father—is committed to, and engaged with, his team of employees. He is constantly and aggressively seeking out what is wrong so he can do what it takes to deliver for his customers.

Mark Sanborn, author of the best-selling book *The Fred Factor* and long-time friend of mine (who knows I am a big fan of St. Elmo's), was dining there on a recent trip to Indianapolis. My friend had a minor problem with his order. He texted me to say that while he loved almost everything about the experience to that point, there was just one slipup.

I immediately dropped Craig an email.

To Sanborn's (and my) surprise, before he could finish his meal, the St. Elmo's team leaped into action. Here's the text I received from my friend:

> Manager on duty came over and said the owner wanted
> to buy me some bourbon. Holy smokes. Btw, I just had
> the best bone-in ribeye I've ever eaten. Seriously perfect.

Certainly, every manager and every restaurant should jump to immediately fix any problem. However, my experience is that many don't want to hear the bad news. (Just look at how few owners or managers respond personally to complaints on social media. I have yet to receive any response to that negative review of the Mexican restaurant that I critiqued online.)

Because Huse encourages his team to look for the negative—and for others to share challenging feedback—they earn positive responses from customers like Mark Sanborn.

St. Elmo's Has a Culture of *Reciprocal Respect*

"My dad genuinely likes, respects, and values the St. Elmo staff—at every level, front of house, back of house, management—everyone," said Craig Huse. "Because of him, it's as natural as breathing for me."

"We provide an opportunity for service staff to earn a real income and we support them with training, business cards, making them the stars of the show—similar to professional sports and entertainment where the athlete or performer is highlighted. And we have group health insurance, short-term disability options, 401(k) plans, years of service recognition programs and events.

"Having seven-year old twins of my own (Sophia and Carson), I understand the sacrifices people in our industry make to work and provide for their families," Huse continues. "Nights, weekends, schedules constantly being adjusted to meet guest demand—all of these are taxing on the children and spouses of our service professionals. I'm certainly much more sympathetic to this reality and grateful for their commitment."[77]

My experience has been that the team at St. Elmo's— among the longest tenured staff at any restaurant I've ever visited—have great respect for Craig Huse because of the great respect he has for them.

ICONIC SUCCESS

Managers and staff have bad days and employees fail to deliver for customers on occasion. I'm certain that St. Elmo's is no different.

However, no small part of their achievements spring from the perspective that they bring to their business. "My father—Steve Huse—and I refer to all of us as *stewards*. We are here guiding this iconic steak joint through a period of time, with the goal of leaving it in a much better place than when we arrived. Stewardship versus a job or an investment leads to a lasting legacy. St. Elmo belongs to the city of Indianapolis. We are simply its stewards," Craig Huse told me.

Consider the thousands of elegant restaurants in the United States—hundreds alone in just in midtown Manhattan, for example. Yet, according to a report in *Restaurant Business Magazine,* this single location on Illinois Street in Indianapolis is the nineteenth top-earning establishment in America.[78] (Raking in $21.3 million in 2017, St. Elmo's had higher gross sales than New York City's Tavern on the Green or 21 Club.[79]) St. Elmo's isn't just a distinctive Midwestern restaurant. They're an iconic business that can teach any organization about the Five Factors that are the message of this book:

1. **Play Offense**
2. **Get Promise and Performance Right**

3. **Stop Selling**
4. **Go Negative**
5. **Reciprocal Respect**

Not Even Iconic Businesses Are Perfect

Every business has problems. Even ones who proclaim—like Nokia's CEO—they "didn't do anything wrong" make mistakes. None of the organizations or leaders in this book are perfect.

Some, like the Fairmont Scottsdale Princess, are rapidly ascending. More, like St. Elmo's, are sustaining and enhancing their position. Others, like United Airlines, are trying to reestablish their status. However, they are all attempting to be at the forefront of customer attraction and loyalty. They have expanded profitability while positively engaging their employees. All must keep striving to enhance their execution in order to be considered esteemed and relevant organizations.

- It's not about longevity. Whether you are just launching your enterprise—like Dave and Wyndee Forrest—or you've been around since the early 1900s—like St. Elmo's Steakhouse, you can be an iconic organization.
- It's not about size. You don't have to be Amazon to become iconic. (Even *it* started small!)

- It's not about location. You don't have to have a pristine piece of property like the Fairmont Scottsdale Princess to attract customers.
- It's not about glitz and glamour. As we've seen, you can be a chimney sweep and establish an iconic business—and even became a millionaire.
- *It's all about what you **do**. . . and **how** you do it.*

When you create distinction in your industry and apply the five factors you have studied here, you can join the rare group of iconic leaders who are the future of business.

My wish is that you do.

Endnotes

Chapter 1

1 Rob Haskell, "Disney CEO Bob Iger on Taking the Biggest Risk of His Career," *Vogue*, April 12, 2018, https://www.vogue.com/article/bob-iger-disney-ceo-interview-vogue-may-2018-issue.

2 Jim Rohn, "Success Must Be Attracted, Not Pursued," *Success Magazine*, September 4, 2016, https://www.success.com/article/rohn-success-must-be-attracted-not-pursued.

Chapter 2

3 Serena Ng, "P&G to Shed More Than Half Its Brands," *Wall Street Journal*, August 1, 2014; https://www.wsj.com/articles/procter-gamble-posts-higher-profit-on-cost-cutting-1406892304.

4 Greg McKeown, *Essentialism: The Disciplined Pursuit of Less* (New York: Crown Business, 2014), 16.

5 David Edelstein, "Blockers Is a Raunchy Farce That's Fundamentally Sweet," *Vulture*, April 5, 2018, http://www.vulture.com/2018/04/blockers-review.html.

6 Cheryl L. Grady, Anthony R. McIntosh, M. Natasha Rajah and Fergus I. M. Craik, "Neural correlates of the episodic encoding of pictures and words," Proceedings of the National Academy of Sciences of the United States of America, March 3, 1998, http://www.pnas.org/content/95/5/2703.

7 "Mastering Omni-Channel B2B Customer Engagement," Forrester Research (commissioned by Accenture Interactive and SAP Hybris), October 2015, https://www.accenture.com/_acnmedia/Accenture/Conversion-Assets/DotCom/Documents/Global/PDF/Digital_3/Accenture-Mastering-Omni-Channel-B2B-Customer-Engagement-Report.pdf (emphasis mine).

Chapter 3

8 Liz Hilton Segel, in an interview for "Playing offense: What it takes to drive growth," McKinsey.com, March 2017, https://www.mckinsey.com/business-functions/marketing-and-sales/our-insights/playing-offense-what-it-takes-to-drive-growth.

9 Catherine Clifford, "How Amazon founder Jeff Bezos went from the son of a teen mom to the world's richest person," CNBC; October 27, 2017, https://www.cnbc.com/2017/10/27/how-amazon-founder-jeff-bezos-went-from-the-son-of-a-teen-mom-to-the-worlds-richest-person.html (emphasis mine).

10 Peter King, "His Career Forged in Darkness, Eagles Coach Doug Pederson Ready for Spotlight of Super Bowl 52,", *Sports Illustrated* MMQB, January 28, 2018, https://www.si.com/nfl/2018/01/29/doug-pederson-philadelphia-eagles-super-bowl-52-brett-favre-peter-king.

11 Laura Morgan Roberts, Gretchen Spreitzer, Jane E. Dutton, Robert E. Quinn, Emily Heaphy, and Brianna Barker, "How to Play to Your Strengths," *Harvard Business Review*, January 2005, https://hbr.org/2005/01/how-to-play-to-your-strengths.

12 Bob Glauber, "Super Bowl LII: Doug Pederson's aggressive coaching makes him the toast of Philadelphia," *Newsday*, February 5, 2018, https://www.newsday.com/sports/columnists/bob-glauber/super-bowl-eagles-doug-pederson-1.16548722.

13 Ibid.

14 Sophie Quinton, "The Economic Case for Paying Your Cashiers $40K a Year," Citylab.com, March 20, 2013, https://www.citylab.com/life/2013/03/economic-case-paying-your-cashiers-40k-year/5037/.

15 Ibid (emphasis mine).

16 Ibid.

17 Ben Parr, "7 Ways to Capture Someone's Attention," *Harvard Business Review*, March 3, 2015, https://hbr.org/2015/03/7-ways-to-capture-someones-attention.

18 Gordon Tredgold, "7 Truths About Accountability That You Need To Know," Inc. Brand View, Inc.com, September 14, 2017, https://www.inc.com/gordon-tredgold/7-truths-about-accountability-that-you-need-to-kno.html.

19 Peter Bregman, "The Right Way to Hold People Accountable," Harvard Business Review, January 11, 2016,

https://hbr.org/2016/01/the-right-way-to-hold-people-accountable.

20 Kim Harrison, "Why employee recognition is so important—and what you can do about it," "Cutting Edge," Cutting Edge Public Relations, https://cuttingedgepr.com/free-articles/employee-recognition-important/.

21 Tobias J. Moskowitz and L. Jon Wertheim, "Does Defense Really Win Championships?" Freakonomics.com, January 20, 2012, http://freakonomics.com/2012/01/20/does-defense-really-win-championships/.

22 Ibid.

Chapter 4

23 William J. McEwen, "Promises, Promises," *Gallup Business Journal,* November 19, 2001, http://news.gallup.com/businessjournal/169/promises-promises.aspx.

24 Christopher Koch, "Looks Can Deceive: Why Perception and Reality Don't Always Match," *Scientific American Mind,* July 1, 2010, https://www.scientificamerican.com/article/looks-can-deceive/.

25 Jenna McGregor, "Stepping out of Steve Jobs' shadow, Tim Cook champions the promise of Apple,"*Chicago Tribune*, August 15, 2016, http://www.chicagotribune.com/bluesky/technology/ct-tim-cook-apple-20160815-story.html.

26 Kevin Tofel, "Love it or hate it, 97% of Apple Watch customers are satisfied in product survey," ZD Net, July 20, 2015, https://www.zdnet.com/article/apple-watch-satisfaction-survey-results/.

27 Facebook posting from John T. Howard; used with permission

28 Julia Belluz, "The SEC charged Elizabeth Holmes, CEO of Theranos, with fraud," Vox, March 14, 2018, https://www.vox.com/science-and-health/2018/3/14/17120606/theranos-sec-charges-fraud-elizabeth-holmes.

29 Ibid

30 Zoe Kleinman, "Uber: The scandals that drove Travis Kalanick out," BBC News, June 21, 2017, http://www.bbc.com/news/technology-40352868.

31 "Our Story," Kasita.com, https://kasita.com/our-story/.

32 "The 25 Most Disruptive Companies of the Year",' *Inc.* Magazine, https://www.inc.com/profile/kasita.

33 Chris Weber, "Introducing Uber Health, Removing Transportation as a Barrier to Care," Uber Newsroom, March 1, 2018, https://www.uber.com/newsroom/uber-health/?state=V6IhuDwdOAL5idTuQnGDWQoZyw3XGZYD7aHb_S6OQeA%3D&_csid=iGbUjU7kRTc0zIwu-puGXg#_.

34 Ayelet Gneezy & Nicholas Epley, "Worth Keeping but Not Exceeding: Asymmetric Consequences of Breaking Versus Exceeding Promises," Social Psychological and Personality Science, May 8, 2014, http://journals.sagepub.com/doi/abs/10.1177/1948550614533134 (emphasis mine).

35 Ibid.

Chapter 5

36 Ian Altman, "How to Sell Like an Expert, Not Like a Salesperson," Inc.com, https://www.inc.com/ian-altman/how-to-sell-like-an-expert-not-like-a-salesperson.html.

37 Leigh Ashton, "Sales Is Not About Selling," NASP.com, http://www.nasp.com/article/B37B4EC2-D838/sales-is-not-about-selling.html (emphasis mine).

38 Philippe Aussant, "6 Stats That Show How the Customer Experience Impacts Your Bottom Line," iPerceptions.com, June 14, 2017, https://www.iperceptions.com/blog/customer-experience-statistics (emphasis mine).

39 Interview with Lynn Vojvodich, "The Customer Experience Journey," McKinsey & Company, December 2014, https://www.mckinsey.com/business-functions/marketing-and-sales/our-insights/marketing--sales-the-customer-experience-journey.

40 Ibid

[41] Gary Vaynerchuk, "The One Thing I Didn't Clarify Enough in *Jab, Jab, Jab, Right Hook*," *Gary Vaynerchuk blog*, 2016 https://www.garyvaynerchuk.com/the-one-thing-i-didnt-clarify-enough-in-jab-jab-jab-right-hook/.

[42] Ibid.

[43] Daniel Cressey, "Brain Scans of Rappers Shed Light on Creativity," *Nature*, November 15, 2012, https://www.nature.com/news/brain-scans-of-rappers-shed-light-on-creativity-1.11835.

Chapter 6

[44] Sarah Elizabeth Adler, "The Power of Negative Thinking," *Atlantic,* Jan/Feb 2018, https://www.theatlantic.com/magazine/archive/2018/01/the-power-of-negativity/546560/#2.

[45] John Humphreys, "Weakness or Opportunity," MIT *Sloan Management Review,* Spring 2007, https://sloanreview.mit.edu/article/weakness-or-opportunity/.

[46] Jennifer Kaplan, "The Inventor of Customer Satisfaction Surveys Is Sick of Them, Too," *Bloomberg News*, May 4, 2016, https://www.bloomberg.com/news/articles/2016-05-04/tasty-taco-helpful-hygienist-are-all-those-surveys-of-any-use.

[47] Frederick F. Reichheld, *The Loyalty Effect: The Hidden Force Behind Growth, Profits and Lasting Value* (Boston: Harvard Business School Press, 1996).

[48] Ibid.

[49] Daniel Schneider, Matt Berent, Randall Thomas, and Jon Krosnick, "Measuring Customer Satisfaction and Loyalty: Improving the 'Net-Promoter' Score," June 2008, http://www.van-haaften.nl/images/documents/pdf/Measuring%20customer%20satisfaction%20and%20loyalty.pdf.

[50] Andrew J. Elliot and Marcy A. Church, University of Rochester, and St. Mary's University, "A Motivational Analysis of Defensive Pessimism and Self-Handicapping," *Journal of Personality* from Blackwell Publishing, June 2003, http://persweb.wabash.

edu/facstaff/hortonr/articles%20for%20class/elliot%20self-handicapping.pdf.

51 Joaquín Selva, "The Upside of Defensive Pessimism: The Potential Benefit of Anxiety," *Journal of Positive Psychology*, August 14, 2017, https://positivepsychologyprogram.com/defensive-pessimism/ (emphasis mine).

52 Ibid.

53 Ibid.

54 Dan McGowan, "Nalli: St. Vincent Adapting by 'Disrupting Ourselves,'" *Inside Indiana Business*, May 8, 2018, http://www.insideindianabusiness.com/story/38142783/nalli-st-vincent-adapting-by-disrupting-ourselves (emphasis mine).

55 Jason Boog, "Elon Musk: 'Pay attention to negative feedback, and solicit it, particularly from friends'," *Adweek*, March 21, 2013, http://www.adweek.com/digital/elon-musk-pay-attention-to-negative-feedback-and-solicit-it-particularly-from-friends/.

56 Bill Murphy, Jr., "Why Every Leader Should Try Jeff Bezos's Infamous 'Question Mark Method'," Inc.com, June 1, 2017, https://www.inc.com/bill-murphy-jr/customer-service-jeff-bezos-question-mark-rule.html.

Chapter 7

57 Bernard Marr, "Why Great Employees Quit." CNBC.com, February 27, 2017, https://www.cnbc.com/2017/02/27/why-great-employees-quit.html (emphasis mine).

58 Christine Porath, "The silent killer of workplace happiness, productivity, and health is a lack of basic civility," Quartz.com, September 15, 2017; https://qz.com/1079344/the-silent-killer-of-workplace-happiness-productivity-and-health-is-a-lack-of-basic-civility/.

59 Ibid, (emphasis mine).

60 Ibid.

61 Amy Adkins and Brandon Rigoni, "Managers: Millennials Want Feedback, but Won't Ask for It," Gallup, June 2, 2016,

http://news.gallup.com/businessjournal/192038/managers-millennials-feedback-won-ask.aspx.

[62] "100 Best Companies to Work For" *Fortune*, http://fortune.com/best-companies/.

[63] Jessica Dickler, "These are the best places to work in 2018," CNBC.com, December 6, 2017, https://www.cnbc.com/2017/12/05/the-10-best-companies-to-work-for-in-2018.html.

[64] "Salesforce: Great Places to Work Review," Great Place to Work Institute, 2018, http://reviews.greatplacetowork.com/salesforce.

[65] "Wegman's: Great Places to Work Review," Great Place to Work Institute, 2018, http://reviews.greatplacetowork.com/wegmans-food-markets-inc.

[66] Nathan Gotch, "How to Fire a Toxic Client," Gotch SEO, https://www.gotchseo.com/how-to-fire-a-client/.

Chapter 8

[67] Antoine Gara, "Jorge Paulo Lemann Says Era of Disruption in Consumer Brands Caught 3G Capital by Surprise," *Fortune*, April 30, 2018, https://www.forbes.com/sites/antoinegara/2018/04/30/jorge-paulo-lemann-says-era-of-disruption-in-consumer-brands-caught-3g-capital-by-surprise/#4721bca51f9b.

[68] Adam Lashinsky and David Meyer, "Steel Twist, Facebook Privacy, Autonomy Conviction," *Fortune* CEO Daily, May 1, 2018, http://fortune.com/2018/05/01/steel-tariffs-whatsapp-privacy-autonomy-conviction-ceo-daily-for-may-1-2018/.

[69] Lauren Dixon, "3 Steps to Align Culture with Business Strategy," *Talent Economy*, August 31, 2016, http://www.talenteconomy.io/2016/08/31/3-steps-to-align-culture-with-business-strategy-3/.

[70] Ibid.

[71] Linden Brown, "10 steps for HR: how to build a strong customer culture," *Inside HR,* November 17, 2015, https://www.insidehr.com.au/10-steps-to-building-a-customer-focused-culture/.

72 Feann Torr, "'No reason' for dieselgate class action, says VW," Motoring, November 8, 2017, https://www.motoring.com.au/no-reason-for-dieselgate-class-action-says-vw-109733/.

Conclusion

73 Antoine Gara, "Jorge Paulo Lemann Says Era of Disruption in Consumer Brands Caught 3G Capital By Surprise," *Forbes*, April 30, 2018, https://www.forbes.com/sites/antoinegara/2018/04/30/jorge-paulo-lemann-says-era-of-disruption-in-consumer-brands-caught-3g-capital-by-surprise/#11bda62f1f9b.

74 https://www.stelmos.com/about/history/

75 Jill Phillips, "5 Questions: St. Elmo's Craig Huse strives to carry on tradition," *Indianapolis Star*, January 25, 2014, https://www.indystar.com/story/money/2014/01/25/5-questions-st-elmos-craig-huse-strives-to-carry-on-tradition-/4894795/.

76 Kyle Inskeep, "The Suite Life: St. Elmo Steak House," Fox 59 News, February 19, 2018, http://fox59.com/2018/02/19/the-suite-life-st-elmo-steakhouse/.

77 Ibid.

78 "The Top 100 Independents," *Restaurant Business Magazine,* 2017, http://www.restaurantbusinessonline.com/top-100-independents.

79 Liz Biro, "2 more steakhouses are coming to Downtown Indianapolis," *Indianapolis Star*, September 12, 2017, https://www.indystar.com/story/entertainment/2017/09/07/2-more-steakhouses-coming-downtown-indianapolis/641878001/.

Acknowledgments

Extraordinary thanks to my friend and publisher, Jonathan Merkh. It was an honor to have worked with you through the years—and it's even more of a privilege to reunite under your imprint at Forefront Books.

Thanks as well to Geoffrey Stone. Your insight and gentle hand through the editing process has been appreciated from my first book to this latest one.

This book would not have happened without the dedication and belief of Shelley McKain Erwin, chief operating officer of the Distinction Institute and Distinctive Presentations. Shelley makes it all happen—from coordinating my crazy schedule to all things design and Internet-based. And the fact that she's the world's greatest sister is pretty cool too.

I also appreciate the others in our small organization—especially the work of Benjamin Amick, who edits video and audio, contributes to our website, helps keep the wheels on the business, and does an all-around great job.

Thanks, too, to Perry Cremeans for his diligent efforts for so many years.

Each year in Las Vegas, the Ultimate Business Summit is held to provide entrepreneurs the opportunity to grow their business and themselves. My partners and friends, Larry Winget and Randy Pennington, make this a professional privilege and personal delight. I'm grateful for the opportunity to work together with such terrific pals.

I am indebted to my clients at corporations and associations across the nation and around the world. In addition, I want to express my appreciation for the amazing people at the speakers bureaus who keep my calendar full.

Jason Bradshaw at Volkswagen Group Australia is an incredible client and remarkable friend. Thank you for the opportunity to share with your team and learn from your significant expertise.

Thanks, too, for the friendship and dynamic leadership I've experienced with Michael Bartsch, managing director of VW Group Australia. His innovative concepts—like positioning the service department at the front end of the dealership—have provoked much of the thought you see reflected here.

Jack Miller at Fairmont Scottsdale Princess is the epitome of leadership. You have endured tragedy, engaged your team, excited your community, and exuded the positive spirit the world needs. Thank you for allowing me to be a small part of that.

Craig Huse of St. Elmo's was kind to share his insights about my favorite restaurant in America. I appreciate both his willingness to participate and the extraordinary experiences I've enjoyed as a customer of his for many years.

Thank you to my colleagues in Speakers Roundtable. It is such an honor to join you as a part of the most esteemed association of individuals in professional speaking.

There are so many pals in the world of professional speaking and publishing that I'm reticent to name any individuals for fear of accidentally excluding someone! I will make special mention of Scott Stratten in thanks for our Speak and Spill group of speakers. Scott's friendship is extraordinary—and he has brought together a highly diverse and remarkable group of professionals who have become great friends. Thanks, Scott, for adding so much to the texture of my life through these wonderful associations.

I would like to extend a special note of gratitude to the great guys and consummate professionals that I am so honored to call friends—the Oak Ridge Boys. I first met these amazing men in my teens, and they still inspire me to this day. Joe, Duane, William Lee, and Richard—and road manager, Darrick—I am grateful for your friendship.

Heartfelt appreciation to the best buddies a guy could have—my pals in the band, Diamond Rio. Thanks to Brian Prout, Dana Williams, Gene Johnson, Jimmy Olander, Dan Truman, and Marty Roe. You guys rock! (But not too much—you're a *country* band!)

My gratitude as well to the many authors and speakers who have given me ideas and assisted in the development of the concept of this book.

My deepest appreciation, too, to my two stepsons, Corbin and Faron, and Corbin's wife, Amber, and their newest additions to our family, young Calvin and Lydia!

Finally, my heartfelt gratitude to my wonderful wife, Tammy, for being such a loving and gentle presence in my life. It's great being teammates through life together with you.

Finally, last but certainly not least, thanks to *you,* the reader, for taking your time to absorb *Iconic.* I sincerely hope it will be of value to you.

Dedication

In chapter 3 of this book, I recounted the story of how I was wowed by my friend, Gerard Mauvis, who devoured my book *Create Distinction* and then asked, "What's next?" That was the question that inspired the writing of this book.

Gerard was an enthusiastic supporter—and implementer—of the principles of creating distinction and growing into iconic status. Alongside his leader and close friend, Jack Miller, Gerard gave his all into growing the Fairmont Scottsdale Princess from a respected resort into a globally iconic property.

Gerard also delivered to my wife and me some of the greatest customer experiences that we've ever had. He truly "walked his talk" and was one of the most consistent leaders whom I've ever had the privilege of knowing.

In September 2016, Gerard Mauvis tragically lost his life in an accident. He left behind a wonderful wife, Marlee, and sons, Will, Harrison, and daughter, Demi.

Following the tragedy, Jack Miller said, "Gerard's zest for life, his love of family and friends, and his contributions to our resort, community, and industry will be missed. I personally feel a loss of partnership as he was so much a part of what we have created over the past five years. Although we are saddened, we have the deep joy of remembering his love of life and adventurous spirit. Rest in peace, dear friend." These are my sentiments exactly.

With deep appreciation and humble respect for his memory, I dedicate this book to Gerard Mauvis in thanks for his integrity and his inspiration.

Scott McKain
May 1, 2018
Las Vegas, Nevada

About the Author

Scott McKain's experiences have been diverse and remarkable.

From playing the villain in a Werner Herzog movie that esteemed film critic Roger Ebert named as one of the fifty great movies in the history of the cinema, to being inducted into the Professional Speakers Hall of Fame, from having been chosen (along with Zig Ziglar, Dale Carnegie, and Seth Godin) to be one of about thirty members of the Sales and Marketing Hall of Fame, to a decade as a globally syndicated television commentator on the entertainment scene, it's not a stretch to say Scott McKain's life has been distinctive.

He has spoken on platforms in all fifty US states and twenty-one countries. His audience members have ranged from a president on the White House lawn to farmers in a small hut with a dirt floor in Brazil. His clients include the icons of global business: SAP, Cisco, Apple, VW, Fairmont, CDW, Canyon Ranch, and many more.

He is the founder of the Distinction Institute and is one of the most requested and iconic professional speakers in the world.

He and his wife, Tammy, live in Las Vegas, Nevada.

FOR MORE INFORMATION

We would love to hear—and share—your stories about iconic organizations and leaders! Visit IconicBusinessBook.com and join our community!

If you would like more information on creating distinction and becoming iconic, access our resources at: DistinctionNation.com. You'll find videos, white papers, and even a free audio training course on how to create personal distinction. It's all there for you.

Join leading companies like Apple, SAP, BMW, Cisco, CDW, Lilly, and many more—have Scott McKain speak to your next event!

Contact Shelley@ScottMcKain.com for more information — go to ScottMcKain.com — or, call us at +1-800-838-6980. We would love to work with you to make your next meeting iconic!

OTHER BOOKS
BY SCOTT MCKAIN:

ALL Business Is Show Business!

What Customers REALLY Want

Create Distinction
(originally published as *The Collapse of Distinction*)

Seven Tenets of Taxi Terry

ALL Business is STILL Show Business!
(15th Anniversary Edition)